Oil Painting

From Van Eyck to Rothko

Oil Painting

From Van Eyck to Rothko

by
Jean-Luc Daval

SKIRA

RIZZOLI
NEW YORK

© 1985 by Editions d'Art Albert Skira S.A., Geneva

Published in the United States of America in 1985 by

RIZZOLI INTERNATIONAL PUBLICATIONS, INC.
597 Fifth Avenue/New York 10017

Reproduction rights reserved by A.D.A.G.P. and
S.P.A.D.E.M., Paris, and Cosmopress, Geneva

Printed in Switzerland

12-89   LA 2200

Library of Congress Cataloging in Publication Data

Daval, Jean-Luc.
    Oil painting from Van Eyck to Rothko.

    Translation of: La peinture à l'huile.
    Bibliography: p.
    Includes index.
    1. Painting—Technique. I. Title.
ND1500.D3713   1985   751.45   85-42920
ISBN 0-8478-0628-6 (U.S.)

Contents

Introduction

Because for five centuries it was the medium of the best-known master-pieces, the technique of oil painting became synonymous with painting itself. Earlier techniques like encaustic and tempera fell into oblivion, and later ones like watercolour and pastel, which developed during its hegemony, were overshadowed. But oil painting too has a history. It came into being at a definite time, and it grew and changed in response to the needs of artists and the evolution of art.

The study of the past shows that each period works out the media best suited to its aims and requirements. So it was with the oil technique. It appeared in the fifteenth century, when painters were intent on rendering optical illusions in order to make their art more convincing. To the linear experiments in spatial representation which came to be known as perspective, oils added an indispensable complement by permitting depth to be suggested through light and colour. Once taken up, oils were found to offer artists an unsuspected range of possibilities in keeping with their growing aspirations, till the time came when the illusionist powers of this new binding medium merged with the painter's facture. With a Rembrandt, a Frans Hals, a Velazquez, the oil technique becomes identified with the very expression of their genius: only pigments ground with oil, then thinned or thickened, could impart such intensity to their brushwork.

The oil technique has become so closely identified with the idea of painting that it is not always realized to what extent the twentieth century—which no longer sees the picture as a window or a mirror—has departed from it and taken to new media like collage or acrylic, as better suited to contemporary demands.

While the greatest names of painting figure in it, this book is not one more history of art. Its illustrations, and the many details they include, are meant to bring out the specific qualities of the medium and show the painting in a new light. The focus on details permits the picture to be read at the distance from which the artist painted it—the distance of his bent arm or his hand plying the brush. The reduced size of the reproduction, in the result, closes up the real gap that existed between the painter's eye and the surface of the canvas. And it is in close-up that the brushwork and paints yield their full savour.

Technique changed with changing ways of seeing. It also changed when the work answered a different purpose or when the artist claimed a different status from that of the craftsman. Further: paintings as we see them now in the museums are often different from what they were when they were made. Time and history have acted upon them. The paints are a living thing; they alter with age, they mellow or decay, or man steps in and renews them or brings them up to date, reframing or censoring the picture, darkening or diluting the sensitive film of pigment.

Today's techniques of scientific analysis enable us to penetrate beneath the surface of the picture, but they cannot fathom all its mysteries, and the methods and formulas of Jan van Eyck, for example, are still a riddle. Scientific analysis and restoration, important as they are, engender a clinical scanning of the picture, favourable to identifications but emptied of that pleasure of seeing and doing which we hear about from artists and their friends. The best works are a triumph over the chaotic and shapeless, and the picture lover's keenest aim is to reach back to the creative moment

◁ **Jan van Eyck**
(c. 1385/90-1441)
Marriage Portrait of Giovanni Arnolfini
and Giovanna Cenami, detail, 1434.
Oil on panel.

when imagination was transmuted into line and colour. Through the study of his technique we can overhear the dialogue between the artist and his work, for the paints are the medium of his creation, they are the physical reality through which the viewer can enter into communication with the maker.

Giorgio Vasari, himself a painter, wrote the first history of art. He was the first writer to explain the revolution in handling and seeing brought about by the invention of oil painting. In the first edition of his book, *Le vite de' più eccellenti architetti, pittori et scultori* (Florence, 1550), he credited the invention to Jan van Eyck. In the introduction he gives what is already a modern definition of the picture: "A painting is a plane surface covered with colours and running lines; it may be a wooden panel, a stretch of wall or a strip of canvas." And he concludes: "The work should attain perfection without any appearance of effort, without the spectator feeling any of the pangs suffered by the painter in making it." The creative artist has so often concealed the miracle of his achievement behind the perfection of its workmanship that a closer look at his technique should permit us to recover something of the initial thrill.

No artistic skill is neutral or non-committal. Each technique has its specific scope and powers which cause it to be chosen or indeed invented when previous techniques reach a point where nothing new can be expected of them. Being rare, the invention of a new medium is all the more significant. The art of painting as we know it reposes on a tradition, direct and unbroken, going back to antiquity and indeed to Egypt. A tradition so long, so rich, that the young artist, from boyhood, went through an apprenticeship of many years (thirteen years in the case of Cennino Cennini, a contemporary of Van Eyck and author of a famous treatise) in order to initiate himself into all the craft skills that have ensured the permanence of the Old Masters' work.

Every painting, whatever the technique, calls for a ground and priming, for pigments mixed with a binding medium and appropriately thinned, for a varnish or protective coating. These different materials are interdependent. Colour pigments changed little or not at all up to the beginning of the nineteenth century; they had been arrived at by experience, by trial and error, before the advances of chemistry offered new ones. It was solely the composition of the medium or vehicle that went to define the different techniques by modifying the physical properties of the colouring matter. On the nature of the colours depended the choice of ground and varnish. Taking these materials, the greatest artists have used them with variations of their own, yielding unexpected effects. The purpose of this book is to illustrate the innovations they made in technique and handling, and consequently in ways and range of seeing.

From the earliest times wood was used as the ground for easel paintings (i.e. portable paintings), until oils called for canvas. Priming was needed to make the coats of paint adhere and to protect them from below. This priming, or undercoat, directly determined the tonal quality of the painting. Not all pigments are suitable; the plant pigments so widely used in cloth-dyeing were found to be unusable in painting, because impermanent and often incompatible with each other. Mineral pigments, whether natural like earth colours or chemical, have different reactions according to the binding medium and thinner used; they may be transparent or opaque, bright or mat, to an extent that makes their base unrecognizable. On the binding medium depend the effects of light refraction and reflection, the thickness of the paints and the time they take to dry.

The oils used in painting are of two kinds, fixed oils and essential oils. The first are pressed chiefly from linseeds and poppy seeds; they dry very slowly, gradually solidifying. The essential oils are extracted from plants like lavender or resinous balsams like turpentine; these spirits dry by evaporation.

The monk Theophilus, in his medieval treatise on the arts and crafts (c. 1110-1140), describes the grinding of pigments in oil. Cennino Cennini in his *Libro dell'Arte* (c. 1400) also recommends oil for the preparation of colours, in particular for glazing and varnishing. So Jan van Eyck (c. 1385/90-1441) was not the inventor of oil painting, as Vasari claims. He did, however, perfect it so decisively that tempera was thereby superseded as the usual medium for fine paintings. Also and above all, Jan van Eyck lived and worked at a time when artists were rising from the craft level and gaining a higher status, when painting too was gaining a wider range of applications. As heirs to a long tradition, painters were intent on developing their art in response to new aspirations. This is reflected in the writings just mentioned. Theophilus' book is that of a practising craftsman, with detailed accounts of methods and recipes. So is that of Cennino Cennini; but, while referring back to Giotto as the "most accomplished" of artists, he shows a new, forward-looking sensibility. Cennini introduces the idea of evolution in the arts, an idea inseparable from the history of oil painting.

While summing up the knowledge and studio practice of his time, Cennini, writing in Florence or Padua around 1400, describes the actual training of a painter and emphasizes the necessity for him to arrive at an individual manner of painting with respect to both other artists and to nature. He thus opened a debate which still continues: "This is the art that one calls painting, and for the practice of it you must have imagination in order, by the operation of the hand, to find out things unseen (hidden in the shade of the natural) and to record them with the hand, demonstrating that what is not may be."

With this definition, the history of modern painting begins. It will be illustrated here by the artists who have marked it with an imprint of their own. Their aspirations and advances will be described in terms of their own practice and testimony and those of their contemporaries, and their distinctive character will be brought out by comparison with the work of others.

Master of Flémalle
(probably Robert Campin,
c. 1378/79-1444)

The Virgin and Child before
a Firescreen, detail, c. 1420-1425.
Oil on panel.

10

The oil technique was a
most wonderful invention, and a great
improvement in the art of painting.
Giorgio Vasari, 1550

Artists of the fourteenth century had already tried to render the picture space more complex by expressing depth in terms of certain optical experiences. But it was not till the fifteenth century that they succeeded in making the picture resemble a "window opening on the world." Painting became illusionistic, the eye setting the scale of this fiction. As measured by the standards of sight, the world was reduced to the human dimension. Space became homogeneous and painting offered the viewer a slice of reality.

The early experiments with linear perspective, whose most conspicuous effect was to distort the parallel lines perpendicular to the picture surface, which were made to converge on the vanishing point, were worked up into a geometrical system by the Italians, from Masaccio to Piero della Francesca, by way of Alberti and Uccello. At the same time artists were searching for a pictorial technique capable of giving the illusion of atmospheric depth and achieving aerial perspective. This was only made possible by oil painting and its transparent colours, as introduced by the Flemish master Jan van Eyck. He was the first to create effects of depth. The secret of Van Eyck's methods is lost, but other Flemish masters took them over, and the Italians too experimented with them as soon as they realized how much more luminous the picture could be made by means of them.

Vasari is the first writer to point out the paramount importance of the new technique. In the introduction to the first edition of his *Lives* (1550), he wrote: "The oil technique was a most wonderful invention, and a great improvement in the art of painting. Its first discoverer in Flanders was John of Bruges [Jan van Eyck] ... He was followed by his disciple Roger of Bruges [Rogier van der Weyden] and Hans [Memlinc] ... The procedure was introduced in Italy by Antonello da Messina."

Some points are questionable in Vasari's account, such as Antonello's alleged journey to Flanders, but in describing the invention, in his life of Antonello, he goes into some detail: "Meanwhile the Fleming John of Bruges, a painter much esteemed in his country for his skill, set out to try different kinds of colours. A man of inquiring mind, keenly interested in alchemy, he tried out these oils in preparing varnishes and other ingredients. One day, after having taken great pains in painting a picture, he varnished it and according to custom put it out in the sun to dry. Unfortunately, because the sun was too hot or because the wood was not seasoned enough, the panel split. Seeing the harm caused by the sun, John resolved to devise some way of avoiding such mishaps in future. Being dissatisfied both with the varnish and the process of tempera painting, he set himself to find a kind of varnish which should dry in the shade, to avoid having to put his pictures out in

the sun. After many experiments with various mixtures, he found at last that linseed oil and nut oil, among the many he tested, were more drying than all the rest. From these therefore, boiled with other mixtures, he obtained the varnish which he, and indeed all the painters of the world, had so long desired. Further experiments showed him that when the colours were mixed with these oils they were not only water-resistant but had more lustre without the aid of any varnish; and besides, what seemed more wonderful to him, the colours blended better than in tempera." Vasari dates this invention to the year 1410. He goes on: "The fame of this discovery soon spread not only through Flanders but to Italy and other parts of the world, and great desire was aroused in other artists to know how he brought his works to such perfection... The pictures, however, especially when freshly painted, had that strong smell which mixing oil with colours gives them, so that it would seem the secret might have been discovered. But for many years it was not." In his study of the origins and evolution of oil painting (*La Découverte de Jean van Eyck*, 1947), the Russian scholar Alexander Ziloty points out a number of earlier references which go to confirm Vasari's account: Bartolomeo Facio in 1454-1455, Antonio Filarete in 1464, Vespasiano da Bisticci at the end of the fifteenth century, and Marcantonio Michiel between 1515 and 1543. All of them refer to the advances made in oil painting by Van Eyck and the Flemings.

But towards the end of the eighteenth century Vasari's account was questioned by several scholars, on the strength of scientific arguments and a systematic study of the early treatises on painting which were then beginning to be translated and published. These showed that painters had been familiar with oils since antiquity and made abundant use of them in the Middle Ages. Thus G. E. Lessing (1774), J. F. L. Mérimée (1830) and others, from a reading of the texts rather than the pictures, challenged the long-standing view of Van Eyck as the inventor; but they fail to explain the new effects which he achieved, and above all they can adduce no other inventor of the oil technique which revolutionized the art of painting. Ziloty (1947) confirms Vasari's account with scientific arguments and demonstrates where Van Eyck's innovation lay: the use of a diluent extracted from an essential oil.

This seems the most plausible view. It accounts for the influence which Van Eyck exerted and above all for the consequences which it had. True, it is not till more than half a century after Van Eyck, in the writings of Leonardo da Vinci, that we find the first reference to the diluent employed, spirits of turpentine (by then commercially marketed). But there is no reason why Van Eyck, an adept of alchemy as Vasari tells us, could not have used it already.

11

Tempera had been the standard technique for panel painting. Cennino Cennini in his craftsmen's handbook (c. 1400) gives an account of tempera as practised by contemporary Italian painters. The pigment ground with oil is applied by means of a water-egg emulsion; this covering coat was better suited to flat areas of colour than to light effects. For gradations the painter had to use the three-shadings technique described by Cennini: "Take three vessels. In one of them put pure red, for example. Of the other two, one will have a lighter colour, and the third will be for halftones made up from the first vessel and the second lighter one. Now take the first, which is the darkest... follow the folds of the figure in the darkest places and never go beyond the middle..." Cennini also recommends the use of oil for coloured glazings and varnish.

With tempera, space was represented only by effects of volume and the contrast of darker and lighter colours. Oil, on the contrary, created an aerial perspective by the transparency of the colours; light appeared to be diluted by the atmosphere and a great sweep of depth could be suggested. A volatile diluent reduced the viscosity of the oil, and this fluidity permitted the finest details to be rendered and thinned out the coats of paint. Where lights are required, the white underpainting is allowed to show through, and blendings are obtained by superimposed coats. The presence of a resin in the binding medium intensifies the colours, makes the final coat of varnish superfluous, and imparts to the picture an extraordinary glow and freshness.

Only the substitution of a volatile diluent for the water-egg emulsion can explain the sensuous luminosity and transparency of the paints achieved by Van Eyck. Like his predecessors, he used colours ground in oil, boiled or even polymerized to make it more solid and transparent. To the colours he might have added resins blended with volatile spirits which would evaporate after diluting the paints. This technique would call for a building-up in successive scumbles similar to that of watercolour painting.

Jan van Eyck
(c. 1385/90-1441)
The Madonna of Chancellor Rolin, c. 1433-1434.
Tempera and oil on panel.

Vasari, himself a practising painter thoroughly familiar with the different media, accurately defines the limits of tempera and the advantages of Van Eyck's oil technique. Referring to the former, he writes in his life of Antonello da Messina: "It was well known that tempera lacked a certain mellowness and vividness which would have given more grace to the drawing and more glow and smoothness to the colouring. Tempera painting was always done by means of hatchings laid in with the tip of the brush. For all the efforts made by many artists to improve this technique, they failed to discover the right recipe, even by mixing liquid varnish with the tempera... They still lacked any means of fixing the images on a panel with the same solidity as on a wall, nor was it possible to wash them without carrying away the colour or to make them resist knocks which inevitably occur when one is handling pictures." In the introduction to his *Lives*, where he describes the invention of oil painting, Vasari points out its advantages: "This procedure enhances the colours. All it asks of the artist is care and love, for oil in itself possesses the property of making colour smoother, softer, more delicate, and more easily harmonized and shaded."

Tempera, then, because of its opacity, permitted of only a limited range of effects. Oil came as the revelation of a suppler, richer, softer medium, capable of optically reproducing a surprising diversity of textures. With it, the paints were so smoothly blended that the brushwork was no longer visible. Van Eyck apparently used the technique of three gradations described by Cennini (for it was still being used by Rubens), but he was able to fuse them before the coat of paint hardened or to interpose them by a play of under-layers and over-layers thanks to the transparency of his medium. Van Eyck's tones have retained their peculiar glow and intensity because he never mixed black and white with his colours. With age, the values have a tendency to fuse the tones with which they are mixed. With him, as in the watercolour technique, modelling is obtained by transparency, dilution and superimposed layers of paint.

Fra Angelico
(1387-1455)
The Deposition, detail
of the right side, 1437-1440.
Tempera on panel.

Jan van Eyck
(c. 1385/90-1441)

The Madonna of Canon Van der Paele,
1436: detail of the foot of St. Donatian's
archiepiscopal cross and the tiled floor.
Oil on panel.

Fresco painting in the mid-fifteenth century was the standard technique for high art, thanks to its solidity and the look of simplicity and directness that stems from its necessarily rapid execution—rapid because each day's work must be completed before the wet plaster ground has had time to dry. Michelangelo preferred fresco to all other techniques because it met his "titanic" requirements. Yet Cennini was already aware of the advantages of tempera for panel painting: "Know that this work is truly fit for a gentleman, for he can do it clad in velvet!" Once oil painting appeared, however, its superiority was recognized. Its solidity was unquestionable. It was better adapted to the naturalistic illusionism gaining ground in the fifteenth century. There seemed no limit to its range of effects, to its power of rendering depth. It lent itself to reworking, whereas fresco allowed of no correcting.

◁ **Jan van Eyck**
(c. 1385/90-1441)
St. Barbara, 1437.
Brush drawing in brown
on panel coated with gesso.

▷ **Gerard David**
(c. 1460-1523)
Altarpiece of Jean des Trompes,
detail of the central panel with
the Baptism of Christ: Plants on
the river bank between Christ
and the angel, 1502-1508.
Oil on panel.

Art historians have long been fascinated by Van Eyck's beautiful little St. Barbara panel in Antwerp. A minutely detailed brush drawing rather than a painting, does it represent the preparatory stage of an unfinished painting? Or was it meant to stand as a picture in its own right? For after all it is signed and dated 1437. This panel is one of the few of its time to reveal the underpainting and show how the artist prepared his composition.

Cennini describes how to prepare the wooden panel and Van Eyck seems to have followed the exact stages indicated. "The panel should be of well-chosen linden or willow wood, free of any defects." (Van Eyck's *St. Barbara* is on an oak panel.) It should be primed with "six successive coats" of a glue made from parchment clippings boiled in water. "When you have laid on the glue, take an old canvas of fine white linen, cut or tear it into strips, soak these in the glue and spread them over the flat surface of the panel." This canvas covering was meant to keep the panel from splitting. Cennini covers it next with eight coats of fine gesso mixed with warm glue. After drying, the panel is ready for polishing with a pumice stone. "The gesso having been rubbed down and polished till it looks like ivory, you should draw upon it with charcoal of willow wood or with the lead pencil or else a silverpoint. Draw with a deft hand, shading the folds and faces. When you have finished drawing your figure (especially if it is a panel by which you set great store, from which you expect profit and honours), let it rest for a few days... Then, with a small pointed squirrel's hair brush, firm up your drawing everywhere." Van Eyck draws with a very fine brown, the Italians with a cooler tone known as *verdaccio*. The drawing is elaborate and precise, for its darks and lights are allowed to show through the fluid paints.

The artist of the fifteenth century worked like the medieval illuminator, on a surface laid down flat. He had no palette. He kept his colours in a series of small jars and broke them down each time into three tints, on a small board, to obtain his modellings. Each colour requiring a brush of its own, the painter laid in like or similar tones over the whole picture, moving from one to the other in the garments, then in the architecture or landscape, finally painting in the faces. This tone-by-tone, layer-by-layer method accounts for the delicacy of the blendings. Details of particular fineness were obtained by a deft pricking with a brush dipped in white for highlights, in pure colour for the shadows.

Hans Memlinc
(c. 1433-1494)

The Shrine of St. Ursula, 1489.
Left to right: St. Ursula and her companions
returning from Basel to Cologne; Martyrdom
of St. Ursula's companions; Martyrdom of
St. Ursula, with Cologne Cathedral in the background; and Virgin and Child with two nuns.
Oil on panel.

A scrutiny of Flemish paintings in a raking light shows that, owing to this method of work, the thickness of the paints may vary considerably. Lighter parts are thinnest, while the darker, more intense areas may number as many as ten layers of paint.

Vasari refers twice to the transmission of Van Eyck's invention or secret (one passage was quoted above): "In his old age he revealed it to his pupil Roger of Bruges [Rogier van der Weyden], who communicated it to his disciple Ausse [Hans Memlinc] and to others already mentioned."

The oil technique suited the Flemings, giving them a means of recording all that their eyes noted and lingered over in everyday life: the glowing beauty of a shaft of light, the fleeting expression of mood or feeling in a face, the sensuous richness of a fabric (Flemish craftsmen were famous makers of cloth and luxury objects). The intimist vision of the Flemish masters contrasted with the more conceptualist vision of the Italians, and Michelangelo's judgment of it as reported by Francisco de Hollanda is significant: "In Flanders they paint only to deceive the external eye. Their painting is of stuffs, bricks and mortar, the grass of the fields, the shadows of trees, and bridges and rivers, which they call landscapes, and little figures here and there. And all this, though it may appear good to some eyes, is in truth done without reason, without symmetry or proportion, without care in selecting or rejecting."

Nevertheless, oil painting was taken up in Italy because it afforded new, exceptional spatial effects and facilitated the artist's work, just as painting was entering one of its greatest periods of exploration. Further, oil painting on panels or objects suited the tastes of the new clientele of art lovers and collectors who were eager to surround themselves with things of beauty and refinement. Till then, painting had been made chiefly for religious purposes, in connection with churches and other buildings. Now, as an independent art form, it served to record the image of real men and to picture events and places known to them or remembered by them. The very fact that in 1434 the Italian merchant Giovanni Arnolfini, established in Bruges, had himself portrayed by Jan van Eyck speaks for the tastes and needs of these patrons—princes, bankers, merchants and so on.

Jan van Eyck
(c. 1385/90-1441)

Portrait of a Man in a Red Turban, 1433,
possibly a self-portrait.
Oil on panel.

Thanks to their commercial and financial acumen, the Italian cities enjoyed an unprecedented prosperity in the fifteenth century, while Rome as the seat of the papacy stood at the centre of international life. Italy multiplied its exchanges with the whole of the known world, and many Italian firms and banks had permanent representatives abroad. Thus the Arnolfini firm of Florence was represented at Bruges by Giovanni Arnolfini, who had his marriage portrait painted by Van Eyck in 1434. Italian admiration for Flemish painting is further shown by Hugo van der Goes' famous Portinari altarpiece, ordered from him by the Medici representative in Bruges, Tommaso Portinari, who about 1480 dispatched it to Florence: this *Adoration of the Shepherds* exerted a fascination on Florentine artists.

In his life of Antonello da Messina, Vasari tells how Flemish painting reached Italy; though somewhat fanciful, his account can be accepted in its main lines. Works by Jan van Eyck were in the possession of King Alphonso of Naples, Federigo da Montefeltro, Duke of Urbino, and Lorenzo de' Medici. But it was Joos van Ghent's *Communion of the Apostles* for the Duke of Urbino and Hugo van der Goes' Portinari triptych in Florence that most directly inspired the Italian painters. Yet, as Leon Battista Alberti noted in his treatise on painting (1435), the Italians were remote from the realism of the Flemings. Alberti emphasizes the role of drawing and composition in recreating the plastic form of man in a space reduced by perspective to the human scale. While Alberti aimed at keeping a balance between the real and the conceptual, he defined an ideal magnificently illustrated by Piero della Francesca. And it was just when Piero was exerting a widespread influence in Italy, in the mid-fifteenth century, that he was impressed by the Flemings, whose style and technique were being made known by Antonello da Messina.

Hugo van der Goes
(c. 1440-1482)

Portinari Altarpiece, right wing:
St. Margaret and St. Mary Magdalene
with Maria Portinari and her daughter Margherita, 1476-1478.
Oil on panel.

**Piero
della Francesca**
(c. 1416-1492)
The Virgin and Child
with Two Angels or
Madonna of Sinigallia,
1470.
Oil on panel.

According to Vasari, Antonello went to Bruges after seeing the Van Eyck painting owned by King Alphonso of Naples. But Antonello was born about 1430 and Van Eyck died in 1441. Probably it was in Naples that Antonello learnt the oil technique, perhaps from the French artists already familiar with it who began working there during the short reign (1438-1442) of René of Anjou, Count of Provence. For the Flemish oil technique had spread southwards through Burgundy and Provence, as attested by the masterpieces of Aix and Avignon. In France Jean Fouquet had already mastered it. In Naples it was Colantonio, Antonello's master, who first ben-

efited from the lessons of these Flemish-influenced French painters and combined the luminosity of the Flemings with the construction of the Italians.

By 1460 Flemish influence was felt throughout Italy. By the 1470s it was a major influence. "The mid-1470s represent a master pivot in the history of modern painting. If one examines the points of marked resistance to the 'harsh' and broken style, it will be found that they are all in the South or can be connected with Piero's zone of influence... It was a Southerner, Antonello da Messina, led for reasons still unclear to travel up the peninsula, who from Naples

23

Jean Fouquet
(c. 1420-c. 1480)

The Melun Diptych, left wing:
Etienne Chevalier commended
by St. Stephen, c. 1450.
Oil on panel.

24

Piero della Francesca
(c. 1416-1492)
Diptych of Federigo da Montefeltro
and Battista Sforza, front of
left and right wings, c. 1472.
Oil on panel.

to Venice awakened a new interest in colour treated as a carrier of light and no longer as a function of drawing. He brought a new stimulus by diffusing the technical recipes of the Flemings" (André Chastel, *Le Grand Atelier d'Italie, 1460-1500*, 1965).

At Urbino, where Joos van Ghent worked for the Duke (c. 1472-1475), Piero della Francesca assimilated the northern vision of the Flemings. He took over their light and space, their careful detail and velvety brushwork, as attested by his astonishing portraits of Federigo da Montefeltro and Battista Sforza. Verrocchio, Leonardo's master, shared this admiration. But it was in Venice, where he arrived in 1475 (possibly after meeting Piero on the way), that Antonello da Messina left his deepest mark. According to Vasari: "He went to Venice where, being greatly addicted to women and pleasure, he determined to settle and end his days. There he painted many pictures in oil, as he had learnt to do in Flanders. His works were much appreciated for the novelty of their technique and execution; they still adorn the houses of Venetian nobles. Others were sent to various places." In a letter of 1476 from Pietro Bon to Galeazzo Maria Sforza, Antonello's work is described as "promising to become one of the most brilliant of all both in Italy

and abroad." Antonello died prematurely in 1479, after having taught "the secret of oil painting" (in Vasari's words) to his friend Domenico Veneziano, who spread it abroad in Florence. In Venice, which thanks to the oil technique was to become one of the foremost schools of sixteenth-century painting, tribute was paid to Antonello in the epitaph inscribed on his tomb: "In this ground is buried Antoninus the painter, the highest ornament of Messina and all Sicily; celebrated not only for his pictures, which were distinguished by singular skill and beauty, but because, with high zeal and tireless technique, through mixing colours with oil, he first brought splendour and permanence to Italian painting."

Vasari ends his life of Antonello with these words: "Thanks to this discovery, artists have progressed to such a point that they have almost contrived to give life to their figures." Today one may go further and say that, by combining Italian vision with Flemish technique, Antonello broke away from the Gothic tradition; he opened the way for modern painting by giving it the power of suggestion and illusion that it required to invent the images in which man and his aspirations could find a fuller radiance and truth.

Antonello da Messina
(c. 1430-1479)

The Virgin Annunciate.
Oil on panel.

Antonello da Messina
(c. 1430-1479)

Portrait of a Man (Il Condottiere), 1475.
Oil on canvas.

Leonardo da Vinci
(1452-1519)

The Virgin and Child with
a Vase of Flowers, detail, 1478-1480.
Oil on panel.

2

The right way of entering into the unfathomable depths of painting.
Palma Giovane, late 16th century

By the end of the fifteenth century the Italian artist claimed for himself a different status from that of the craftsman. For Leonardo, the painter reveals the underlying laws of the world: "Painting is the origin of all arts and crafts, it is also the source of all science... Science considers the quantity, whilst art considers the quality of things, which is the beauty of the works of nature and the ornament of the world."

The Italians discovered oil painting just as tempera was seen to be too thin and mat for nature imitation, and as the dominant fresco technique was entering a crisis. The constraints imposed by fresco painting, which ruled out retouching and limited the light effects, had apparently been overcome when, after about 1450, the pricked cartoon came into use, enabling the painter to work out an elaborate composition independently of the wall. But depth of tone was unattainable and the illusion of space fell short of what the Flemings achieved in oil. Atmospheric effects were ruled out, and standing in an architectural setting the fresco did not, like the independent panel painting, presuppose a spectator in a fixed position determined by the perspective. Leonardo was well aware of this problem, writing in 1492: "There is a general practice of wall painters in a church or chapel which is very blameworthy. They set out a composition with buildings and landscapes on one plane, then higher up another composition in which they change the point of view, and so on. This is perfectly silly."

Indeed, since Giotto the fresco painter had set out his scenes in continuous rows, image after image. As against this, the laws of perspective required the painter to place the spectator at the centre of the visual pyramid described by Alberti, required him in other words to consider the wall as a whole (as Leonardo did in his *Last Supper* at Santa Maria delle Grazie, Milan) or to divide his wall painting into a sequence of independent pictures. The latter solution was adopted by Mantegna in the famous frescoes of the Camera degli Sposi (Mantua, 1474), where he adapted them to the architecture so cunningly as to isolate or frame the different pictures, whose overall effect is that of an eye-deceiving illusionism. Mantegna thus created a fictive, inhabitable space by treating the scenes singly—something he could have achieved more easily on panels, in the seclusion of the studio, than on the scaffoldings of a work site.

Mantegna was the first to use canvas instead of the traditional wooden panel. The earliest painting on canvas is his *St. Euphemia* (Museo di Capodimonte, Naples), dated 1454. It is done in tempera, and thereafter Mantegna made many tempera paintings on canvas. In Venice, where no fresco tradition existed, art passed almost directly from mosaic to oil painting on canvas. The first

extensive sequence of paintings to decorate the Hall of the Great Council in the Ducal Palace was done on canvas in 1480 (destroyed in the fire of 1577).

Panel did not necessarily limit the size of the picture: on panel Titian painted his *Assumption of the Virgin* in Venice (22½ × 11½ ft.), and Rubens his *Raising of the Cross* in Antwerp (15 × 11 ft.). But canvas was now preferred, being lighter and more manageable. Mounted on a stretcher it offered the brush a more congenial ground; being softer and more flexible, it offered textural and gestural possibilities which Titian soon discovered. In Italy the use of canvas coincided with the introduction of oil: this extraordinary conjunction occurred in Venice around 1500.

But oil painting on canvas called for a different priming from that used for tempera. Vasari comments on this difference: "These canvases painted in oil cannot be coated with gesso, for it would crack when they are rolled up. Instead of gesso, they are primed with a mixture of flour and walnut oil, to which a few measures of white lead are added." The trouble with white lead or silver white, which is only a carbonate of lead, is that it tends to blacken. So that what the artist gained in freedom, with the introduction of canvas, was lost in the instability of the paints.

With the Italian painters the egg tempera technique evolved as they multiplied their oil glazes. Then the "secret" of Van Eyck was revealed to them by Antonello da Messina. It was taken up by the Venetians and then through Domenico Veneziano by the Florentines, who developed it in their own way, exploring its possibilities of impasto and opacity. In the hands of the Venetians, oil permitted colour to throw off the tutelage of drawing.

But between the Flemings and the Venetians there was Leonardo. Fascinated by effects of atmosphere and light, he developed the possibilities of semi-liquid colours, deepening the thickness and opacity of certain tones mixed with black or white in varying proportions. Titian inaugurated a new manner of painting: relying on his inspiration and skill, he tackled the picture directly with brush and colour—what he called making "the bed of painting." With him, the painting of a picture became at every stage a creative adventure, uncontrolled by sketch or underdrawing. To his successors he bequeathed a free, untrammelled handling, encouraging the artist to express his feelings freely on the spur of the moment and to profit by chance suggestions coming to him during the elaboration of the work.

For Leonardo, painting was inseparable from observation and reflection. Vasari illustrates this with an anecdote: "It is said that the prior of Santa Maria delle Grazie was very importunate in urging Leonardo to finish the work, it seeming strange to him to see

Leonardo standing half a day lost in thought; and he would have liked him never to have put down his brush, as if it were a piece of work like digging the garden." Leonardo's mind was set, not on plying the brush (his paintings are few and often unfinished), but on thinking out a new vision, which he conveyed as much by the ideas and principles of his art writings as by his actual pictures. While studying every aspect of nature, he was not content with singling out isolated phenomena but sought to embody them in a global, harmonized vision of the world.

Leonardo da Vinci
(1452-1519)
The Adoration of the Kings, 1481-1482.
Yellow ochre underpainting and
brown ink on panel.

Leonardo da Vinci
(1452-1519)
The Virgin and Child
and St. Anne, detail,
1508-1510.
Oil on panel.

Among the problems occupying Leonardo, the expression of depth was foremost. The oil technique, which he learnt in Verrocchio's workshop, gave him a luminosity of colouring which enabled him to work out a new relation between figure and setting. Here, by developing his chiaroscuro, the intricate play of light and shade, he arrived at his famous *sfumato*.

To measure the changes Leonardo brought about in the painter's way of seeing, it is enough to compare his *Adoration of the Kings* (Uffizi) with Van Eyck's *St. Barbara* (Antwerp), both left in the state of a sketch or underpainting. For Van Eyck, line acts as a guide and shadings follow or emphasize the contour. Leonardo, on the contrary, sets less store by line than by the sequence of planes. He steps up the contrast of light intensity between the parts, while close attention to modelling carried him on to flowing passages permitting him to integrate each object into its setting. Shadow was the key to this integration: "Four chief parts have to be considered in the painting, namely, quality, quantity, place and figure. By quality I mean shadow, and that part of it which is more or less dark. Quantity, that is the size of a given shadow in relation to neighbouring shadows. Place, that is the manner in which they should be placed and over what part of the body they fall." The point, for Leonardo, was not to imitate nature but to achieve a harmonious whole compelling the eye to see and the mind to think. With this in view, he refers continually to shadow as being a fundamental feature: "The painter's first purpose is to make a body seem to stand out from the flat surface of the picture... This is the perfection of art and it arises from the right and natural disposition of lights and shadows, which is called chiaroscuro." But colour can enhance the illusion created by chiaroscuro if it integrates the values. This is what Leonardo set out to do, and for this purpose he modified the oil technique taken over from the Flemings.

For one thing, he renewed the underpainting by treating it in terms of planes and darkening it; the lakes and coloured glazes which he

Perugino
(1445-1523)
Apollo and Marsyas.
Oil on panel.

laid over it never wholly cover the under-layers but allow them to show through, creating a subtle atmospheric depth. Further, by painting in lights over darks, he produced unexpected effects of iridescence or, on the contrary, effects of warm luminosity when he laid in a lighter over a darker glaze.

For another, he modified the thickness of the paints by adding white or black to each colour in order to heighten the relief. The semi-liquid colour paste, though reducing transparency, permitted him to work with fresh paints and achieve defter shadings of colour. "In the course of the work," wrote Vasari, "the still fresh colours mix and blend more easily. By this means artists may impart to their figures an infinite grace, vivacity and force. Seeming to be in relief, they look as if they were ready to step forth from the picture."

Perugino, though also schooled in Verrocchio's workshop, kept to the transparency of the Flemings and transmitted it to his pupil Raphael. But while Raphael's early works allow the ground to show through, he was soon prompted to take over Leonardo's impasto as a means of gaining sharper relief. The use of cartoons

helped him to achieve the quality he sought on the level of drawing and composition, but only a suppler medium enabled him to go as far as he did on the level of colour and values. Thin opaque paints favoured his use of gradations and tactile effects. This smoothly blended brushwork was taken over by many subsequent painters, from Poussin to Ingres. Like Leonardo, who mixed black or white into his colours, Raphael began by reversing the thickness of the paint layers. With him, the darks became less thick than the lights, which tended towards impasting and, by the relief thus achieved, found their lustre enhanced by the final varnishing. This latter operation had again become necessary, the artists of the sixteenth century tending to diminish the proportion of resin in favour of spirits in the make-up of their medium, and the viscosity of the oleo-resinous mixture was incompatible with prolonged brushing in fresh paints.

Raphael attained a level of perfection which set a new standard. But (Vasari relates) when Raphael realized that he could not vie with Michelangelo he set out to achieve a supremacy of his own in the representation of space and things, more particularly in

Raphael
(1483-1520)

Portrait of a Woman
or La Donna Velata, c. 1516.
Oil on canvas.

the art of ''painting fine, lifelike heads of women and children.''
The impact made on the Venetians by Antonello da Messina's oil technique can be seen from an anecdote (apocryphal no doubt, but none the less significant) recorded by Carlo Ridolfi (1648): ''Giovanni [Bellini] saw this new manner of painting, in which there appeared a certain blending and softness of the colours unattainable in tempera. Unable to imagine the means adopted by Antonello, he obtained entrance to the latter's house, passing himself off as a gentleman who wished to have his portrait painted, and as he wore a Venetian toga he easily remained unrecognized. And so Antonello, taking no precautions, set to work on it, and Giovanni observed that from time to time he dipped his brush in linseed oil, and so found out the method employed by Antonello.''
Giovanni Bellini, at first a tempera painter, assimilated the technique and space of the Flemings and became the master of a whole generation which, with Giorgione and Titian, put Venetian painting in the foremost rank. The atmosphere of the lagoon city gave

its artists an innate sensitivity to light more akin to that of the Flemings than any other Italian school. For the Venetians, light did more than merely make objects visible and situate them in depth: its glow and shimmer entered into the subject of the painting and qualified its form and aspect.
A pupil of Giovanni Bellini, Giorgione played a decisive part in the rise of Venetian painting. ''He had seen some things of Leonardo's, worked with great depth of shadow but blended and softened, and this manner pleased him so much that all his life he used it and imitated it when painting in oil. A man of most refined taste, he always chose the finest and most various subjects'' (Vasari). This last point is worth noting, for it was the Venetians who renewed the subject matter of painting by making more of contemporary themes. With them, painting moved away from the Bible and mythology. More responsive to nature and life, they rehandled the traditional themes, with an originality that makes it difficult to interpret some of their pictures. What Giorgione's *Concert Champêtre* (Louvre) and *Tempesta* (Accademia, Venice)

were meant to represent is still a matter of controversy. They are best accepted as the fruit of his imagination.

In his account of Giorgione, Vasari emphasizes a point of some importance: "He would never use anything in his works which he had not drawn from life... All he did was done from life, and not in imitation of any manner." In conclusion Vasari says: "Some things he did are so lifelike and others so delicately blended in their shadings that the best painters of the day acknowledged it. They said that he had the knack of breathing life into his figures and rendering the lustre of flesh tints better than any painter in Venice or elsewhere."

Giorgione is said to have been the first painter to dispense with preliminary drawings and sketches for his paintings. He improvised directly on the canvas, relying on inspiration to work out his composition and colour harmony. This has been confirmed by X-ray analysis of the *Tempesta*, which reveals many changes in the composition. But Giorgione's career was so short (he died at thirty-four) that his pupil Titian was able to "equal him and surpass him greatly" (Vasari), and it was with Titian that painting gained a new freedom, with him that the brushwork came to partake of the expression as a whole.

◁ **Giovanni Bellini**
(c. 1430-1516)
Allegorical Scene, c. 1490.
Oil on panel.

Titian
(c. 1490-1576)
and/or
Giorgione
(c. 1477-1510)
Concert champêtre: Lute Player
and Shepherd with two Nude Women
in a Landscape, c. 1510.
Oil on canvas.

◁ **Titian** (c. 1490-1576)

Madonna of the Pesaro Family, 1519-1526.
Left, Bishop Jacopo Pesaro kneeling
before St. Peter and the Virgin and Child;
Right, St. Francis commending
the Bishop's family. Oil on canvas.

▽ Venus and Cupid, detail, c. 1559-1560.
Oil on canvas.

"Let no one suppose that strength of colouring lies merely in the choice of fine colours, of fine lakes, fine blues, fine greens. It lies rather in the right use of them. I should say that over-charming colours are to be avoided, as are over-finished figures. The whole should produce the impression of an amiable firmness. Before all else, avoid that excess of diligence which detracts from everything" (Lodovico Dolce, 1557).

The ideal of the Venetians was the reverse of Leonardo's: painting for them, instead of revealing the laws of nature, was a sensuous response to life and the beauty of the world. Harmony for the Florentines was worked out mathematically on the basis of line; for the Venetians it was the fruit of gracefulness, movement and even chance, arising out of the colour scheme. "A pity that in Venice they don't learn how to draw well," said Michelangelo. But for Titian emphasis on line was the negation of painting; the picture had to develop freely out of the rough sketch; the brush had to respond freely to the promptings of imagination and sensibility. Beauty was a conquest and invention, the outcome of the painter's dialogue with nature and art.

The Venetians renewed the handling of colour. Hitherto tonal values had determined relief; now it arose from the colour harmony. This was already noticed by a contemporary writer on art:

This freer, looser handling of the paints is characteristic of Titian, who thereby opened out the picture space, suggesting a limitless expanse. His manner evolved remarkably during his long career, steadily gaining enrichment from his experience and his ever more searching insight into colour-light. He used painting, not as a medium of storytelling, but as a revelation of all that intuition may bring to light.

From his pupil Palma Giovane as quoted by Marco Boschini (1674), we know how Titian painted. Already using a palette similar to what we know today, he sketched out his picture directly with a full brush, in light colours.

"I have seen him," reported Palma, "lay in bold strokes, given with thick touches of colour, now a clotted mass of pure red acting so to speak as a half-tint, now a mere dab of white. With the same brush dipped in red, black and yellow, he would shape the relief of the lighter parts and by this system brought forth the promise of a rare figure. He would always begin by applying to his canvas a mass of colours, which acted as background to the figures he wished to represent."

The initial sketch then was like a monochrome painting in warm tones; and this underpainting remained perceptible. Its freedom of handling must have been most attractive, for Palma adds: "These

oil sketches of his were so much liked that many wished to have them, out of a desire to ascertain the right way of entering into the unfathomable depths of painting."

Titian never left a picture in this sketch-like state. Palma is quoted as saying: "The master never made a figure at the first attempt... After laying in the groundwork, he would turn his pictures round against the wall and leave them there sometimes for months without looking at them. Then, when he felt like tackling them again, he would examine them with a stern countenance, as if they were his mortal enemies, to see whether he could find fault with them. And as he became aware of anything out of keeping with his discriminating conception of them, like a surgeon he would doctor the patient with no indulgence for the pain he might occasion, perhaps straightening up an arm or perhaps setting the bone

structure back into place... It was by operating in this way, and correcting his figures, that he brought them to such perfect harmony as might be achieved by the beauty of nature and the beauty of art."

It was at this stage that Titian worked up the colour by overlaying glazes of various tints diluted in oil or resins or by scumblings. Palma adds: "But in the end he would usually paint more with his fingers than the brush. The final touches were a matter of wriggling his fingers over the extremities of the carnations, bringing the half-tints nearer each other and fusing one tone into another. At other times, with a rub of his fingers, he would lay in a shadow at some point, to give it force, or some red glazing, like an added drop of blood to give vigour to a superficial expression. In this way he worked up and perfected his spirited figures."

Titian
(c. 1490-1576)

Danaë visited by Zeus
in a Shower of Gold, 1553-1554.
Oil on canvas.

▽ Tarquin and Lucretia, 1570.
Oil on canvas.

Though Titian is probably unmatched as a manipulator of paints, the secret of his art lies rather in his manner of distributing light over the composition as a whole. His so-called "cluster of grapes" procedure amounts in effect to concentrating the lights at specific points, not allowing them to scatter, but on the contrary magnifying them by blending them progressively into the deep shadows where they can enhance each other.

If inspired improvisation was Titian's method, it was continued and extended by his successors, Veronese and Tintoretto. Virtuosity is the hallmark of their painting. In a century and a city intent on decoration and pageantry, pictures invaded every room, every human habitation, and grew to unprecedented proportions. To cope with their orders, artists had to reduce the actual time of picture-making, and Tintoretto is said to have reverted to a tem-

Tintoretto
(1518-1594)
The Finding of the Body of St. Mark,
1562-1566.
Oil on canvas.

pera underpainting to avoid the slow drying of the oils which Titian used for this "bed of painting."

Veronese and Tintoretto gave currency to the use of a strongly coloured ground setting the general tone of the composition. Once this tone and atmosphere had been found, the painter boldly brushed in his contrasting lights and darks and blended them by means of glazes defining the colour of objects, the whole having already been harmonized by the ground toning. Because their paintings were often of monumental size, Veronese and Tintoretto developed a keen eye for the effects produced by distance. Unmatched for their skill, they knew how to obtain the accents whose rightness would make up for their time-saving shifts. While their free handling shows that they knew all the "tricks of the trade," these remained in their hands but practical devices for achieving the theatrical illusionism which they aimed at in their painting, an imagined realm of dreams and passions.

Paolo Veronese
(1528-1588)

The Triumph of Venice,
1584.
Ceiling painting on
canvas.

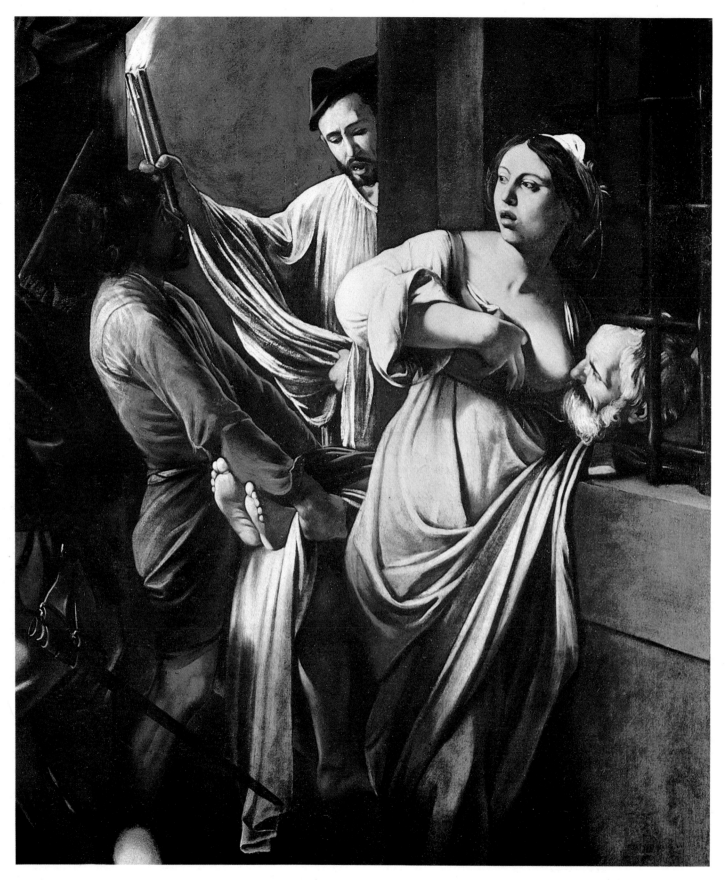

Caravaggio
(1573-1610)

The Seven Works of Mercy, detail:
Woman giving suck to an old man
behind prison bars, 1607.
Oil on canvas.

3

The painter forms without form.

Marco Boschini, 1660

Culture and nature are the two poles of inspiration between which art has always swung. During the sixteenth century painting throughout Italy, except in Venice, was dominated by Mannerism, which may be described as a speculative reference to culture, a style based on an evaluation of the effects achieved by the creators of the Renaissance. In 1548, in his *Dialogo di Pittura*, Paolo Pino saw the ideal as being a combination of "the drawing of Michelangelo and the colour of Titian." This doctrine of eclecticism held the field down to the Carracci (i.e. till the early 1600s), but genuine expression gave way to novelty of manner, fantasies of taste and self-conscious virtuosity. This trend was encouraged by the growth of science. Knowledge of nature progressed so rapidly that it made obsolete the old idea of painting as "experience of reality" which underlay the work of the fifteenth-century painters up to Leonardo da Vinci.

Caravaggio, schooled in the Venetian tradition, reacted against recherché or exaggerated effects and moved back towards nature. His aggressive rejection of Mannerist idealism stemmed naturally from his acceptance of Venetian sensualism. The example he set was decisive for the important seventeenth-century painters who followed him in the direction of realism.

The change brought about by Caravaggio was a change of vision rather than themes (he often kept to religious themes tinged with humanism). Temperamental and overwrought, Caravaggio responded to light and colour in a new way which had immediate technical implications. Responding only to what touched him, to objects and situations which answered to his feelings, he disregarded the traditional hierarchy of art forms and subjects and interpreted directly, forcefully, the dramas and sufferings of existence. Light flashed out of darkness; the body was shrouded in the dimness of common life, a thrall to time and place, but the soul yearned for light.

Caravaggio then did not go to the ancients or the masters for his models, he found them in actual life. Hence the reputation for vulgarity which clung to him and his work for a long time. Legend has it that for his *Death of the Virgin* (Louvre) he painted the figure directly from the swollen body of a prostitute fished out of the Tiber.

Intensely subjective, Caravaggio personalized the art of painting and did away with decorative inessentials. His realism, distasteful to some patrons, appealed to others of a newer, more open-minded generation. Conceived independently of an architectural setting, pictures were purchased more and more by collectors for their own home, to be looked at and lived with and valued more for their pictorial qualities than for what they represented.

Caravaggio, in his ardour and directness, transformed painting into a "living theatre," with him almost autobiographical, where actual experience was heightened and refocused by the play of light and colour. X-ray examination shows that he tackled his subjects directly, and his biographers confirm that he was a fast worker. He was accordingly led to thicken his paints for a more dramatic handling, for intenser effects of light and a more physical, tactile evocation of people and things. With Caravaggio, chiaroscuro found a subjective dimension unknown before. He died in 1610 at thirty-seven, but the admiration his work inspired even in his lifetime is well attested to: "There was no picture gallery worthy of the name, in Rome or elsewhere, which did not covet the honour of owning a canvas by Caravaggio, so much were the hearts of connoisseurs won over to this new manner, all in darkness with a few scattered lights dying away in the shadows" (Bernardo De Dominici).

Rubens was fascinated and influenced by Caravaggio; it was he who in 1607 acquired the *Death of the Virgin* for the Duke of Mantua. The Flemish painter Louis Finson, known to have been in Naples in 1612, took inspiration from him or copied him and made his work known in the North. It was through Ribera, who visited Rome about 1613-1614 when Caravaggio was the rage and settled in Naples in 1616, that Velazquez was made aware of the new Caravaggesque manner of painting.

Released from Mannerism by Caravaggio, painting became the triumphant art of the Baroque period. Welling up from the artist's emotion, colour and light were handled more freely. The Venetian painter and art writer Marco Boschini thus describes the new painting in 1660: "The painter forms without form. With shapeless form he arrives at a new form answering to appearances. He thus achieves an art which may aptly be called painterly." The Baroque age saw the triumph of this loose, painterly brushwork which succeeds so well in conveying the sensuousness of light and colour.

As a painter, Marco Boschini was trained by Palma Giovane in the tradition of Titian, Tintoretto and Veronese. Of colouring, he has this to say: "Sometimes it is given by the impasto, and this is the beginning of the rough sketch. Sometimes it is given by the colour patch and enables the painter to break away from natural objectivity. Or again it is given by the union of colours, and this produces a tender shading; by a dark stroke of the brush, and this conduces to the form of the parts; by a variation in the intensity of the tones, and this produces volumes; by pure and intense colours, and herein lies the art of the brushstroke; lastly, by a glazing which produces the colour harmony."

Peter Paul Rubens
(1577-1640)
The Rape of the Daughters of Leucippus,
c. 1618-1620.
Oil on canvas.

Rubens was one of the most prolific creators in the history of painting. A virtuoso with prodigious powers of work, and a prodigious visual memory, he left an output of some 2500 works. In speed and ease of execution he was unrivalled; his *Kermesse flamande* in the Louvre, a canvas measuring 12½ by 22 feet, with some sixty figures in it, is assumed by Fromentin to have been painted in one day. In a letter to Sir Dudley Carleton (26 May

positions which he then worked up in more detailed sketches. Painting came as the final stage—with him, short and speedy. Over the enlarged design transferred to canvas, he brushed in a transparent underpainting in brown, over a white or grey priming. From that point he exploited all the resources of oil painting, adding spirits and varnish to the boiled oils. Firsthand information about his technique is given by a Swiss doctor, Theodore Turquet de

Peter Paul Rubens
(1577-1640)
Sunset Landscape with Cart.
Oil on panel.

1618) Rubens refers to his *Sarah Driving Out Hagar* (size 5 by 3 feet) as a "mere trifle" requiring less than a day's work.

While he was assisted by pupils and collaborators, it would be a mistake to emphasize their share of the work, so distinctively Rubensian are the many canvases attributed to him. On the other hand, the necessity of saving time and energy, if he was to cope with the demand for his work, led him to renew the painter's technique, to use paints which answered to his mettle while drying quickly and brushwork which yielded brilliant effects with least effort. By birth, taste and schooling, Rubens was a thorough Fleming. He owned ten Bruegels and he inherited the Flemish technique of fluid, transparent paints. But he renewed it by profiting from the example of Titian, whose methods he simplified. His skill, his creative power, his unfailing imagination, all prompted him to improvise.

Rubens drew continually. His studies from nature and life are numerous, but drawing for him was also the direct means of recording the figures of his imagination and roughing out com-

Mayerne, chief physician to James I of England. Rubens painted his portrait and Mayerne observed his procedures and noted them down: "Chevalier Rubens has said that it is necessary when working to mix all colours rapidly with the spirits of turpentine... which is better and not so harsh as spike oil." According to Mayerne, Rubens prepared his siccative oil with litharge: "It is a powerful siccative, so that all colours difficult to dry may be dried by mixing them with some of this oil."

Rubens used a limited range of colours, which he continued to divide into three tints as recommended by Cennino Cennini. But instead of toning his tints with the medium, he added white lead to them, resorting to the modern palette only for the heightening. Rubens' technique is so rich in effects that it has aroused the envy and curiosity of all painters. It is described by J. B. Descamps in his *Vies des peintres flamands* (1753): "It seems that in Rubens' paintings the dark masses are almost entirely devoid of colour... Under his brush everything had at first the appearance of a glaze... One of the chief maxims that he repeated most often regarding

Peter Paul Rubens
(1577-1640)

◁ The Landing of Marie de Médicis
at Marseilles, 162
Oil sketch on panel.

▷ The Adoration of the Magi,
detail, 1624.
Oil on panel.

colour was that it was very dangerous to use black and white. Begin, he would say, by painting in your shadows lightly. See that you do not let any white slip into them, it is the poison of the picture, except in the lighter parts. If once any white blunts that bright and golden point, your colour will lose its warmth and become heavy and grey.''

While he painted wet on wet, Rubens used emphatic heightenings of white to underscore the thickness of the brighter parts.

According to Descamps: ''In the highlights one may lay in the colours to any extent that one sees fit. They have body, yet care must be taken to keep them pure. This can be done by putting each tint in its place, and next to each other, so that a slight mixing with the brush will blend them, fusing them into each other without fretting them, and then one may go back over this preparation and give it those decisive strokes which are always the distinctive mark of the great masters.''

Rubens was particular about his brushes. For impasting he used wide ones, and soft supple ones for blending or overlaying light viscous glazes without disturbing the coat of paint already applied. These brushes with a round, outswelling body and tapering tip "ran rapidly over the picture surface, covering a stretch of drapery at one stroke or contouring a figure with a firm line. No need, as with the flat brush, to go back continually to the palette. The purely manual work of laying in the covering coats was thus done perhaps ten times more quickly" (Maurice Busset, 1929). But such a picture required a long drying time despite the siccative oils used. Rubens' letters prove that he habitually dried his pictures in the sun and delayed delivery for this purpose.

By the fluidity of his colours and the accuracy of his highlights, Rubens achieved a maximum of effects. He practised the direct technique known in Italy as *alla prima* or *fa presto*, which required great sureness in drafting and brushwork. His virtuosity was found

Sir Anthony van Dyck
(1599-1641)
Portrait of Robert Rich,
Second Earl of Warwick,
after 1632.
Oil on canvas.

again in his collaborator Van Dyck and his Dutch contemporary Frans Hals. These new possibilities of transparent shadows and opaque lights also permitted the painter to suggest tactile effects of unexampled richness. Rubens mastered all the resources of the oil technique, and Alexander Ziloty comments: "Words cannot describe his controlled niceties or his sweeping power. All one can say is that the mass of oil colour seems to have been created for him... Rubens' technique henceforth guided painters, like a beacon in the darkness, whenever the need was felt for a painterly renewal of their art. It was his technique, coming by way of Van Dyck, that initiated the flowering of the whole English school in

the eighteenth century. It was his technique again that was to exert a periodic influence on French painting."

Frans Hals accentuated this freedom of execution. He tried out different ways of executing portraits, accurately recording the finest details with a vivacity of touch which grew with age. In his last pictures, with their bold *alla prima* technique, the paints seem to spring into place spontaneously, with an unstudied instinctiveness of their own.

Painting had followed a shifting course between two poles of inspiration: nature and culture. Rembrandt and Velazquez altered its course again by bringing into play the subjective forces of the

Frans Hals
(1581/85-1666)

The Laughing Cavalier,
1624.
Oil on canvas.

artist's personality. This shift occurred on the level of both vision and practice, and its result was a gain in the artist's autonomy. It was in the context of Dutch independence and democracy that Rembrandt gained his: "If I would enrich my mind, I must aim not at honours but freedom," he said. And it was at the punctilious court of Spain that Velazquez gained his autonomy, even while acting as Marshal of the Royal Household. Over and above this

difference of background, one is struck by the similarity of their outlook and the converging advance of their art. Both Rembrandt (born 1606) and Velazquez (born 1599) developed within the "realistic" current initiated by Caravaggio and thereby regained touch with the poetry of everyday life; and both were beholden to the Venetians, known to Velazquez through his two journeys to Italy, to Rembrandt through the pictures he collected. Both men, above all, saw things with their own eyes, searchingly, the picture being for them the spiritualized echo of their personal dialogue with the visible world.

△ **Rembrandt**
(1606-1669)

The Artist in his Studio, c. 1628.
Oil on panel.

▷ **Diego Velazquez**
(1599-1660)

Las Meninas or The Maids of Honour, detail: Self-portrait, 1656.
Oil on canvas.

This fresh confrontation with reality beyond artistic conventions, so natural to them, met with some disapproval. Preferring to work from life rather than from earlier masters, and disregarding the idealism of the Mannerists, they were accused of cultivating ugliness instead of beauty. Their defenders pointed out their attachment to nature and actual life. Thus Francisco Pacheco writes of Velazquez in 1649: "From his childhood my son-in-law Diego Velazquez de Silva received this schooling [in drawing]. He had hired an apprentice, a peasant boy, who sat to him for expressions and various poses... And from this model he did many heads in charcoal and gouache on blue paper, besides many other sketches from life. And in this way he acquired his sureness of hand for portraiture." And of Rembrandt, Joachim von Sandrart said much the same in 1675: "He kept steadfastly to his usual practice and did not shrink from going counter to our rules of art and contradicting them, his view being that one must rely on nature alone and be bound by no other rules. So he handled light or shade and the outlines of things as a work might require, even if they were contrary to the laws of perspective, only provided that they seemed right to him and answered his purpose."

The realism of Rembrandt and Velazquez asserts itself in the very choice of their subjects. They prefer the portrait, or the self-portrait, and when they interpret historical and religious themes one is surprised by their way of humanizing them, by their directness of vision, above all by their manner of painting. In renewing the visual experience of nature, they no doubt distorted it in their own way, for their scrutiny of it was uncompromisingly individual. Contemporary testimony to Rembrandt's "oddities" is to be found in the Florentine art writer Filippo Baldinucci: "This painter... was very extravagant in the style of his painting and evolved in what may be called a wholly personal manner, without detours or limitations, and consisting of violent and reiterated brushstrokes, with a great power of mystery in its way, but with no depth of mystery. And the unaccountable thing is that, despite this way of painting, he worked very slowly... It became common knowledge that anyone wishing to be painted by him would have to sit for two or three months, and few were those who had the patience for it. The cause of his slowness was that, as soon as the initial work was dry, he would take it up again, repainting with big and small strokes, to such effect that sometimes in this or that place the paints were as thick as half a finger."

Rembrandt and Velazquez were the first to attain to a freedom of handling which synthesizes their visual grasp of the world and their spiritual distillation of it in terms of textures and colours. What strikes the spectator, especially in their late work, is the poetry of the paints, independently of any representation. Connected at first with the miniature, from which it issued, oil painting was meant to be seen from close at hand. By the seventeenth

century, lack of finish was being cultivated for its own sake and only made its effects at a distance. The image, as here, was not an imitation of nature but a re-presentation of it. As early as 1620 the poet Quevedo was praising Velazquez for "his distant spots [of colour] which are truth itself, and not merely resemblance." Roger de Piles was similarly struck by Rembrandt. Comparing him with Titian in 1699, he wrote: "These two painters were convinced that there were colours which destroyed each other by overmixing, and so they should be stirred up as little as possible by the movement of the brush... The difference between them is that Titian blended his paints more smoothly, more imperceptibly, while in Rembrandt they are quite distinct when looked at closely, but at

Rembrandt
(1606-1669)

The Jewish Bride,
detail, c. 1665.
Oil on canvas.

52

the right distance they appear to fuse together thanks to the accuracy of the brushwork and the harmony of the colour.''

With Rembrandt and Velazquez the evolution of the oil technique reached its highest point. By the fluidity and glow of their paints, by the freedom of their handling, the painting is given a physical presence whose emotional content heightens the intensity of the initial impression which prompted them to paint. The fruit of a

Diego Velazquez
(1599-1660)
Portrait of the Infanta Margarita,
detail, 1659-1660.
Oil on canvas.

long inner growth and mellowing, the picture reveals itself differently when near at hand or from afar. The painter is directly implicated in what he transmits; his way of painting is inseparable from his way of seeing. Chiaroscuro is no longer a method of staging the scene, but light becomes one with the colour substance and the painting becomes the expression not only of a way of seeing but of a way of being. Hence the impact of these two artists on the Romantics. The young Delacroix wrote in his *Journal* (11 April 1824): "Saw the Velazquez and granted permission to copy it. I am possessed by it through and through. It's got what I've so long been looking for, that firm and yet blended impasto.'' The use of a coloured ground, often red, together with a thick,

Willem Claesz Heda
(1593/94-1680/82)
Still Life, 1634.
Oil on panel.

opaque impasto, led the painters of the seventeenth century towards a darker colour scheme. Baroque art, arising in Italy, needed the contrast with darkness: out of the shadows came the shafts of light suggestive of emotion and spectacle. In Northern Europe, the tradition of brighter, transparent colouring maintained itself, notably in Holland, where it appealed to a new public of well-to-do burghers. Glowing colour ensured the popularity of the re-emerging still life. These still life painters explored the possibilities of denser paints, while continuing to enrich their medium with resins to give a more sensuous lustre to their tactile effects. In the trompe-l'œil "breakfast pieces" of Willem Claesz Heda (two of which were owned by Rubens), reality is given a poetic aura arising from the contemplative calm, order and balance of the composition.

Here the picture is again a mirror image, but the mirage of appearances reposes on a meditative distancing in contrast to the dramatic dynamism of the Caravaggeschi. No one went further in this direction than Vermeer of Delft. With their fine yellows and

blues, and the side lighting in which the subjects are bathed, his pictures are at the opposite pole from Rembrandt. Aloofness and stillness are their hallmark. No door or window is open to let the gaze wander into the infinite. Rather, the interlocking planes of the background seal off the room and the system of lighting steps up the brightness of the pervading tonality. Figures and objects, arranged to a nicety, set each other off in subtle contrasts in which colour prevails over the black and white of values. It is in the half-light, indeed in the very shadows, that tones rise to their highest pitch. Vermeer's palette is governed by the contrast of yellow and blue; his composition is precise, his design tight-knit. He effaces his manner of painting even while identifying it with the texture and light of the elements represented. His fresh, unctuous paints are applied with a fine brush, so smoothly and skilfully as to eliminate any dryness of contour and to expand the points of light. In the intimacy of these closed yet spacious rooms, all is silence, order, intimation. Optical accuracy, instead of dissolving the illusion, gives it a spiritual dimension.

Jan Vermeer
(1632-1675)
Lady seated at the Virginals,
c. 1670.
Oil on canvas.

Nicolas Poussin
(1594-1665)

The Four Seasons: Spring
or The Earthly Paradise, detail, 1660-1664.
Oil on canvas.

The first purpose of painting is to touch us.

Abbé Dubos, 1719

4

"Monsieur Poussin could abide nothing by Caravaggio and used to say of him that he had come into the world to destroy painting. But there is nothing surprising about the distaste he had for him. For while Poussin sought nobility in his subjects, Caravaggio was carried away by the truth of nature as he saw it." So wrote André Félibien in his *Entretiens* (1666-1688). In championing Poussin as against Caravaggio, Félibien shared the views of the Academy which, in France, now stood squarely in the way of the free development of art.

The idea of an Academy was not new; it had attracted artists since the fifteenth century, for as they rose above the status of craftsmen they felt the need to meet together in a club where they could exchange ideas and experiences. But in France it was institutionalized in 1648 with the founding of the Academy of Painting and Sculpture, to which Louis XIV and Mazarin gave real powers of control over exhibitions and teaching. To this, in 1665, was added the Académie de France in Rome, where prize-winning French artists were sent for the purpose of "forming their taste and manner."

In France the authority of the Academy was supreme in matters of taste. It revised teaching methods, replacing the apprenticeship system by drawing courses where art was more talked about than practised. The Academy produced a school of aesthetes rather than studio-trained artists. It imposed intellectual concepts. Painters were expected to appeal to an elite and have its moral backing. Teaching emphasis was on line and composition, colour being held in check. Writings on art, such as Félibien's *Entretiens*, consisted of precepts laid down in a dogmatic spirit. Creative art as conceived by the Academy was dominated by the idea and resulted in a new form of Mannerism: the French Classicism of the seventeenth century.

But this classicism, with its well-defined aesthetic criteria and its constant reference to antiquity, extended well beyond France. Its ideal was shared in Italy by the Roman abbot Gian Pietro Bellori, a fervent admirer of Raphael. In his *Vite de' pittori, scultori ed architetti moderni* (1672) he defends "distinction of taste" in art and criticizes the inclination of the public, who "praise things painted from life because they are accustomed to seeing such things, who appreciate fine colours and not beautiful forms which they do not understand, who grow weary of elegance, look for novelty, despise reason, follow common opinion and depart from the truth of art." For Bellori the "truth of art" was a higher science reserved for cultivated minds; Raphael was its modern exemplar and the ancients were its prophets; they were the models of excellence. Poussin (whom he knew in Rome) embodied Bellori's ideal, and he extolled the allegorical and abstract side of Poussin's art. Noble subjects, presented with style, manner and taste: these were the qualities Bellori sought and defined not with reference to nature but to concepts. Such painting, in which colour played only a secondary role, was all the finer to him for being intellectualized, controlled, geometrized.

"First of all, the subject matter must be noble... And in order to give scope to the painter's display of his mind and skill, it must be made capable of assuming the most excellent form. He must begin by the laying out, then by the ornament, setting, beauty, grace, vivacity, costume, verisimilitude and judgment everywhere," wrote Poussin (letter of 7 March 1665). Félibien (who also knew him in Rome) extolled Poussin for these qualities and urged painters away from the expressive intensity of Rubens and Rembrandt.

The authority gained by the Academy in the seventeenth century caused a break in the workshop tradition. As concepts came to seem all-important, problems of technique and craft were lost sight of. Poussin himself was a victim of this neglect, for his paintings soon began to darken. The French restorer J. G. Goulinat has commented on this: "What was not realized at the time, not even by Poussin, is that the red ochre priming is unsafe. The seventeenth century used it and abused it. The result is... a breaking up and fading away, so that the red shows through more or less everywhere, above all in the glazes."

Theorizing held the field, and various aesthetic doctrines were brought forward and opposed. The views of André Félibien were countered by those of Roger de Piles who, turning for authority to the Venetians and Rubens, opened new paths to French artists. When Watteau was born at Valenciennes in 1684, the town had passed to France from the Spanish Netherlands only six years before. His Flemish background must therefore be taken into account. His imagination had fed on Rubens, and his dreamworld of fancy-dress figures touches the senses more than the mind. But the break in the workshop tradition brought about by the Academy had serious consequences for Watteau. A brilliant draughtsman and fine colourist, he was careless in matters of workmanship and relied too much on improvisation. Disregarding the so long asserted claims of reason, he followed his own bent of grace and sentiment, pointing the way to the Rococo art of the eighteenth century. Turning away from classical models, he looked to nature. His advice to Lancret was "to draw landscape in the neighbourhood of Paris, then to draw figures and so make up from imagination a picture of his choice."

Antoine Watteau
(1684-1721)
The Pleasures of the Ball,
detail, 1716-1717.
Oil on canvas.

Jean-Honoré Fragonard
(1732-1806)
Portrait of a Young Artist.
Oil on canvas.

The imagination and the picturesque: the artist had to rely on these, according to the Abbé Dubos, who voiced the French theories of the Enlightenment. "The *poetic* composition of a picture," he wrote, "is an ingenious arrangement of figures, invented to render the action represented more touching and more credible." But, added the painter Louis Tocqué, "it is the brushstroke that imparts life and movement." And indeed a freer handling of the brush accorded well with eighteenth-century virtuosity and fancy. At the same time it called for a different technique better suited to improvisation and frequent reworking: hence the abuse of thick oil, boiled with litharge and manganese to make it more drying and of pure turpentine as being more volatile. The consequences were noticed in Watteau's lifetime by the dealer Gersaint, who ordered the famous "shopsign" from him. Shortly after Watteau's death in 1721, Gersaint wrote: "It must be confessed that some of his pictures are perishing from one day to the next. They have totally changed colour or are becoming very dirty, and there is no help for it." The Comte de Caylus commented sadly: "Intent as he was on a prompt execution, Watteau liked to paint thick and oily. This device is one of the best... But it requires extensive and careful priming, and this Watteau seldom bothered with. To get the ben-

efit of it, however, when he reworked a picture, he would rub it with thick oil and repaint over that. This momentary advantage had serious consequences in his pictures because he had no care of his colours; he scarcely bothered to change his palette every day, and cleaned it even less; and his pot of thick oil, of which he made lavish use, was full of scum, dust and colours." Hence the cracks, blotches and yellowing that so often mar his paintings.

The same is true of other painters of this period—Fragonard, for example, who gloried in his skill as an improviser and his quickness of hand. On the back of one canvas he proudly wrote: "Frago painted this in one hour." Genius may make light of material obstacles, but the painter's craft is unforgiving. Faulty workmanship shows up sooner or later.

On the credit side is the fact that these painters wisely took over the light-coloured grounds of Rubens. This, and their quick working methods, fortunately led them to use transparent glazes. So that thanks to this lightness their pictures still retain much of their original grace, once the yellowish varnish has been removed.

Diderot, in his famous *Salons*, wrote critical commentaries on the nine Salon exhibitions held in Paris between 1759 and 1781. He was not so much a theorist as a receptive, open-minded amateur,

59

sometimes testy and out of temper with his artists, but often clair-voyant. A picture that moved him he could describe in well-chosen words. So it was with Chardin, whose tactile qualities he responded to. In the *Salon* of 1763 he writes about the *Jar of Olives*: "For this china bowl is real china, and these olives are actually separated from the eye by the water in which they are steeped... Ah, Chardin, what you grind on your palette is not this

colour or that, red, black or white, but the very substance of things. You dip your brush in air and light and spread them over your canvas... There is no accounting for this magic. These thick coats of colour are applied one over another, and the undercoats are allowed to show through. At other times the effect is like a vapour blown over the canvas; elsewhere, like a light foam cast over it... Come close, and everything runs together, flattens out, disap-pears. Step back, and everything is created and reproduced."
Chardin searchingly explored the suggestive possibilities of the paints, identifying them poetically with the objects they represent, and creating a dense and harmonious atmosphere in which the still life gained a new prestige.

His contemporary and rival, J. B. Oudry, though a painter of less searching powers, wrote an interesting account of the mysterious workings of the pigments. A lecture given at the Academy, it is entitled "Reflections on the manner of studying colours by com-paring objects with each other." Oudry shows a new sensibility to white, and he tells how he acquired it from his master Largillière. "Go and fetch a bunch of flowers, all white ones, Largillière told me. I complied at once. When I had set them up in front of me, he came and took his place. He set them against a light-coloured background and began by pointing out to me that, on the shad-owy side, they were very dark against this ground, and that on the brighter side they stood out above in half-tints, for the most part

Jean-Baptiste Siméon Chardin
(1699-1779)
The Jar of Olives, 1760.
Oil on canvas.

animal, you must begin by impasting with full-bodied colour, applied to the principal masses. As these masses are built up, you must indicate each part of them and work them out as thoroughly as possible, laying in tint over tint, but only a little at a time. The pigments, thus nourished, gradually become unctuous and acquire a certain strength. At that point you take the more pliable brushes... and adding a dash of spirits of turpentine which makes

fairly bright. Then he approached the white of my palette to the bright of these flowers, which was very white, and this made me realize that my palette white was still whiter. He made me see at the same time that, in this bunch of white flowers, the brighter parts calling for pure white paint were in no great quantity as compared with the parts remaining in half-tints."

To attain greater luminosity, Oudry advises against the orchestration of colours in depth and recommends surface effects: "A well-made sketch should, in a word, be rather like an overall half-tint, ready to receive the lights and darks, like the grey or blue paper on which one draws." But effects of clotted paint also call for great skill, which Oudry describes with precision: "To paint a furred

the pigments more fluid, you begin working up the details. The limpidity of your colour facilitates this work and gives it all the desired lightness, at the same time precluding any dryness: because you are free to mix it with the undercoats so far as you think fit, and to fuse it with or slip it over this sound and creamy under-painting... The latter has this advantage, too, that it keeps the work in all its lustre: because when the turpentine has evaporated, the colours are left in all their purity."

In eighteenth-century England, aesthetics was a subject of much discussion, bearing on taste, pleasure and imagination. With the rise of the English School, two distinct tendencies can be singled out, represented by Reynolds and Gainsborough.

Sir Joshua Reynolds was a skilled, if careless, technician and a quick worker. When he set up his London studio in 1752, at twenty-nine, on his return from Italy, he could paint a portrait in four hours. Like the Venetians, he dispensed with any preliminary sketch or outline. Working on a canvas primed with white paint, still wet, and using a palette restricted to white, lake and black, he would produce a likeness in grisaille, this at the first sitting, in less than an hour. Afterwards he coloured the grisaille and finished the picture with glazing.

But, from his abuse of bitumen and his habit of reworking with a thick, greasy oil, many of his pictures have cracked badly, the drying time between coats not having been respected. "This over-sight on the part of Reynolds, a great painter thoroughly familiar with the old techniques, reduced his immense knowledge to almost nothing. He mixed varnish with his paints and his contemporaries marvelled at the brilliance and transparency of his colouring. Unfortunately the portraits of his best period soon began flaking, even in the artist's lifetime. Powerless to do anything about it, in the end he declared philosophically: The best painting is crackled" (Maurice Busset).

In contradistinction to Reynolds, Thomas Gainsborough looked to nature rather than the Old Masters. A superb manipulator of the paints, he achieved the most refined and the most gorgeous effects, especially in silks and satins and their deep folds. He used

Thomas Gainsborough
(1727-1788)
Lady Alston, early 1760s.
Oil on canvas.

fine-grained canvases primed with yellow or pink, which he allowed to show through. He then roughed out his figure in mauve, worked up his paints, and went over them with a light scumbling or glaze. He was an inveterate correcter and retoucher. It is said that every night before going to bed he marked in chalk the alterations he wished to make the next day.

Reynolds, though temperamentally out of sympathy with him, could not help admiring his work: "It is certain that all those odd scratches and marks which, on a close examination, are so observable in Gainsborough's pictures, and which, even to experienced painters, appear rather the effect of accident than design—this chaos, this uncouth and shapeless appearance—by a kind of

magic, at a certain distance, assumes form, and all the parts seem to drop into their proper places, so that we can hardly forbear acknowledging the full effect of diligence, under the appearance of chance and hasty negligence."

For greater speed and lightness, Gainsborough worked with liquid paints thinned with turpentine—paints so thin and liquid that his palette ran over unless he kept it on the level. He had an innate sense, not only of effect and artifice, but of lyrical brush-work.

In his remarks on the practical aspects of painting, contained in his Academy lecture, J. B. Oudry warned artists about the quality of the materials which, by now, in the first half of the eighteenth

Jean-Baptiste Greuze
(1725-1805)
Young Girl mourning her Dead Bird.
Oil on canvas.

century, were being marketed by colour merchants. How right he was can be seen today from the cracking and yellowing of much eighteenth-century painting, due to poor varnish and poorly primed canvas.

The grace and gaiety of Rococo brought on a moral reaction as the century advanced. Diderot's *Salon* of 1765 reflects this growing disapproval: "The debasement of taste [in Boucher], of colour, composition, figures, expression and drawing, followed step by step the depravation of manners." To gay life pictures and *scènes galantes*, Diderot opposed the moralizing genre scenes of Greuze. The latter's *Young Girl mourning her Dead Bird* aroused his enthusiasm: "See how true are the details of these fingers and dimples, of this languor and this blushing cheek whose pressure has coloured the tips of these dainty fingers, and the charm of it all... Delightful, delightful!"

The smooth paints of Greuze were a reaction against the sprightlier brushwork of Rococo, but his soberness was that of a precisian intent on the anecdote and forgetful of essentials. Diderot's sympathy with Greuze is indicative of this change of taste, the intrinsic qualities of the painting being less appreciated now than descrip-

tive externals and sentiment. In his *Salon* of 1765 he responds to the story suggested by the picture, a story whose beginning and ending it is for the spectator to invent from the episode pictured; he is more interested in what the picture suggests than in what underlies it. This art of allusion and storytelling, with its leaning towards the picturesque, marks a failure of painterly understanding. The quality of the work was judged by its subject. The artist was lost sight of behind his models, and the painting had to be either picturesque or historical.

As against this art in which subject matter was paramount, there arose a new, robuster current of realism promoted by Goya. It called first of all for acute observation, this taking precedence over painting effects. In his oil study of the Infanta María Josefa, Goya gives a magnificent illustration of the relationship which the modern portraitist was to maintain with his sitter. His aim was to look and see, uncompromisingly, beyond any preconceived ideas, beyond any mere desire to please or charm. Goya sought the truth. Searching into the sitter's features for her character and personality, he set down his reading of them with a forceful brush and glowing colour.

This head was the preparatory study for the fourth figure from the left in the group portrait of the *Family of Charles IV* (1800-1801). The portrait study of María Josefa is one of Goya's masterpieces, both for the sustained intransigence of his vision and the accuracy of its effects of light and texture. Compared with those of Van Eyck and Leonardo, this sketch is seen to mark a further evolution in the painter's craft. Essentials are recorded economically with a few brushstrokes in the right place against the coloured ground. Sensation is identified with the freedom of handling that conveys it so tellingly.

The neglect of painterly qualities in favour of subject matter culminated in the Neo-classicism of the late eighteenth century. The antique ideal came alive with the astonishing archaeological discoveries at Herculaneum (from 1738) and Pompeii (from 1748).

Francisco Goya
(1746-1828)
The Infanta Maria Josefa,
1800.
Oil on canvas.

It was promoted by the evolution of taste represented by Diderot, and by the "moral" regeneration which set the stage for the French Revolution.

Joseph-Marie Vien was one of the first artists to espouse the antique or classicizing ideal. He was so impressed by the discoveries at Pompeii that he seems intent on turning Roman reliefs into French painting. Vien's pupil David had an even stronger passion

Joseph-Marie Vien
(1716-1809)
The Cupid Seller, 1763.
Oil on canvas.

for classical sculpture; he set himself to return to nature "by way of antiquity in the raw." But David's antiquity was inevitably seen through the eyes of Corneille and the latter's exaltation of the ancient virtues. David's gifts and determination soon put him at the head of the Neo-classical school.

With the French Revolution and its aftermath, he became a political artist. He put forth his full strength in the portraits and figure compositions bearing on contemporary history, and Napoleon gave him many opportunities to treat such themes. His *Coronation of Napoleon* is both history painting and reportage. After attending and observing the ceremony (held in Notre-Dame in 1804), David—as Goya had done for his *Family of Charles IV*—made individual sketches and studies of the many persons present. These, with easy mastery, he assembled and fitted together in the final canvas to grandiose effect.

To Delacroix, David seemed the last possessor of the great technical secrets of the past. Though Academy teaching had weakened the studio tradition, the masters had continued none the less to associate their best pupils with their own work. The Revolution, in which David played an active political role, closed the Academy and those secrets were left untransmitted. The post-revolutionary Academy taught only drawing, composition and history.

David, while a thorough craftsman, neglected effects which seemed to him superfluous and subordinated everything to line and precision of design. "David does not draw with the colours

and rarely practises full brush painting. He draws first in reddish brown or more often in *terre de Cassel*, builds up the shadows lightly in bistre, and then covers the canvas, working towards the harmony and values which he fixes at the last moment" (J. G. Goulinat).

Luckily the practitioner in David prevailed over the theorist. He believed in a smooth paint surface unruffled by passion, but his own sensibility was too strong for him, and in the *Coronation*, for example, he achieved effects of light and texture which are all the more telling for their very sobriety.

Gros was one of the first to react against the neo-classical impassiveness which David advocated. Romantic turbulence is already stirring in Gros who, for all his admiration for David, his master, voiced his dislike of what he called "painting in the Spartan style."

Delacroix, an even richer temperament, was against it too. In his *Journal* he notes: "In this school [of David] the rough sketch is non-existent, for one cannot give this name to mere scumbles which are only a slightly more concerted underdrawing, completely covered afterwards by the painting." He goes on to criticize their use of shadows: "The colouring in David is fairly accurate. But what about those tones that Rubens produces with a forthright and virtual colouring, with bright greens, ultramarines, etc.? David and his school think they can produce them by using black and white to make blue, and black and yellow to make green...

Jacques-Louis David
(1748-1825)

The Coronation of the Emperor Napoleon
and the Empress Josephine in the Cathedral
of Notre-Dame, Paris, on December 2, 1804,
detail of Josephine.
Painted in 1806-1807.
Oil on canvas.

Their work, if compared with a picture coloured like those of Titian and Rubens, is seen to be what it really is: ashen, drab and lifeless.''

With Géricault, even before Delacroix, the full brush came into its own again, but the painting remained very fragile. The study of the Old Masters, and the copying of them, were not carried far enough to reveal the secrets of their masterly handling.

This was felt, and the effort to return to the sources was made by editing, translating and publishing some of the early writings on painting technique. The medieval treatise of the monk Theophilus was first published by Lessing in 1774, that of Eraclius by Raspe in 1781; the Lucca manuscript was first published in Italy in 1739, and Cennino Cennini's valuable treatise in 1821. Further editions and translations followed, and painters referred to them for practical information and craft recipes.

The liberating impulse brought by Géricault was clearly felt and described by David's pupil E. J. Delécluze (1855): ''In the *Raft of the Medusa* Géricault developed a subject not only modern but topical. The condition of the castaways ruled out any concern with the beautiful... As the work had some undeniable qualities, it thereby had the effect of showing up the abuse that some of David's pupils had made of their master's principles. And so it happened that Géricault's *Medusa*, held up by the younger men as the soundest, most vigorous expression of his methods, marked the turning of the tide against the exiled David... But the fact is that Géricault acted simply with the idea of imitating nature.''

Théodore Géricault
(1791-1824)
The Raft of the Medusa,
first sketch, 1818.
Oil on canvas.

▷ **Antoine-Jean Gros**
(1771-1835)
Bonaparte at Arcola, carrying the Tricolor
and leading the Grenadiers across the Bridge, 1796.
Oil on canvas.

J. M. W. Turner
(1775-1851)

Light and Colour (Goethe's Theory):
The Morning after the Deluge, Moses
writing the Book of Genesis.
Exhibited at the Royal Academy in 1843.
Oil on canvas.

5

*A new art is still going on,
and always will go on, from where
the Old Masters left off.*

Théophile Thoré-Bürger, 1863

The nineteenth century brought many changes in the art of painting, some of them prompted or imposed by a changing society. Expected hitherto to illustrate an order, a scheme of things, external to himself, the artist now felt impelled to investigate other possibilities of being and doing. No longer hedged in by formal schooling and set programs imposed by masters or patrons, he became more inventive and experimental, above all he turned to new subjects. For the first time the artist's supply preceded the art-lover's demand. Art gained in freedom what it lost in compulsion. Tradition and academic teaching had emphasized history painting as the primary art form and drawing as the primary technique. Departing from this dogma, painters looked now to the experience of nature, in other words to landscape and colour. Even in the later eighteenth century they had felt the need for closer contact with reality, and landscape, though not yet recognized as an independent art form, became a subject of study in the form of sketches. Indeed, the Academy encouraged virtuosity in sketching, and improvisation answered to the deeper aspirations of the rising Romantic generation, flying in the face of set rules. Conscious of the technical shortcomings of their training, the Romantics turned to the museums for models and by copying retrieved some of the quality of older painting.

No longer able or willing to make their own materials, artists relied for them on specialized colourmen or manufacturers, all too often giving no thought to the quality of those supplies, and their work has suffered accordingly. For paradoxically the quality of artists' materials declined just as the chemical industry began making real progress, its discoveries being particularly important in the domain of colours.

From antiquity to the eighteenth century the nature of pigments had changed little. Now the palette was suddenly renewed and extended. In 1782 appeared zinc white; it darkened less than silver white but proved less opaque and more subject to cracking when impasted. In 1795 came the discovery of cobalt blue, more stable than any other. By 1828 ultramarine was being produced artificially; real ultramarine used by the old painters, extracted from lapis lazuli, had been very costly. In 1829 appeared cadmium yellow, so stable that it soon supplanted other yellows. In 1838, emerald green, and in 1839 cobalt violet, the first unmixed violet and remarkably permanent. These were followed by cadmium red, titanium white and others.

On the whole, however, what colour gained in stability it lost in permanence owing to the demands of industrial production and marketing. The mechanical grinding of pigments had been current since 1800, but not till 1838 was it adapted to fine artists' colours by the French manufacturer Blot. Till then each colour had been ground with a due percentage of oil known to the artist. Now standard preparations came into use, and to ensure a greater appearance of freshness to the ready-made colours, linseed oil, whose drying power was highest of all, was replaced by oil of cloves, to which was added spermaceti or paraffin to keep it liquid still longer.

Artists had generally bought powdered pigments stored in glass bottles. Now that the colourman was selling colours ready for use, these had to be supplied in a suitable container, at first in skin bladders— apt with use to ooze or even burst, and to be generally messy. They were replaced by a brass syringe, patented in England in 1824 (and invented in the first place to safeguard Prussian blue and red lakes, which deteriorated in a bladder once it was perforated). Finally, in 1841-1843, the London firm of Winsor and Newton began marketing the colour tube, light, handy and similar to what we know today. Though open-air painting had of course long been practised, it was made easier now by the collapsible tin tube.

This colour as squeezed from bladder or tube was more buttery and less transparent. When laid on it showed the mark of the brush. Such relief effects appealed to painters, who gave up the soft brush for the short bristle brush or the palette knife as better suited for the manipulation of thicker paints. Canvases became standardized—made of strong, specially woven linen, prepared for painting by priming, stretched tightly and tacked over a chassis or stretcher frame, and obtainable in uniform sizes. From the mid-nineteenth century, canvases primed with a white ground were being employed by artists, who preferred a rough grain, as better holding and setting off the brushwork, and a more absorbent ground. They also used cardboard and paper primed by the colourman. Conscious of the errors committed in the past, they turned back to the idea of rapid execution, at one go, as required by the study of nature, and it was this method of work that triumphed with the Impressionists.

Add to this, in the middle and later years of the nineteenth century, the influence of photography and Japanese prints on both the painter's way of seeing and his technique, and it will be realized why and how the art of painting underwent such radical changes. The study of light, beginning in England with Turner (born 1775) and Constable (born 1776), brought a deeper understanding of colour and colour effects, with momentous consequences on the style and practice of painting. The scientific study of colour led to

John Constable
(1776-1837)

◁ Branch Hill Pond, Hampstead,
Evening, c. 1822.
Oil on paper.

▷ Landscape with Double Rainbow,
dated 28 July 1812.
Oil on paper, laid on canvas.

fundamental discoveries: Newton, by passing it through a refract-
ing prism, had broken down white light into the colour spectrum;
Chevreul worked out the laws of colour contrasts; Maxwell put
forward his electromagnetic theory of light; Rood did fundamental work on the optical mixture; and Goethe developed a theory of
colour in which he revealed its psychological, symbolic and phy-
siological aspects.

Turner's *Light and Colour (Goethe's Theory): The Morning after
the Deluge* (c. 1843) refers directly to Goethe's *Farbenlehre*,
translated into English by Sir Charles Eastlake in 1840, and more
particularly to his table of polarities in which yellow was already
associated with warmth and light, and blue with shade and cool-
ness. For Turner, darkness was the prelude to light. In his later
work, he made light the very subject of his paintings: no more
striking example than the *Morning after the Deluge* where the

iridescent bubbles almost form a chromatic circle. Technically
speaking, Turner's innovations were no less decisive, even though
he founded no school. He had begun by raising watercolour to the
level of oil painting, after reintroducing into it the traditional coloured ground of oil painting. Then, having perfected the use of
pure colour in his watercolours, he introduced it into oils, which
he plied with an amazing, unsuspected fluidity. Extending his
palette to the colour prism, Turner arrived at an unprecedented
freedom of handling, resorting simultaneously, sometimes reck-
lessly, to brush, palette knife, hatchings, streakings, stipplings and
so on, even overlaying his oil paints with watercolour glazings or
ink heightenings. But his painting was the living embodiment of
his vision and experience. After all, he had had himself lashed to
a ship's mast in order to observe a storm at sea. Intent more and
more on the visionary and the infinite, he disregarded detail for the

whole; he broke loose from the visible and concentrated on the reality of the painting, the reality of colour, light and matter. In this he was the first modern. Equally modern is the unfinished aspect of his pictures, and also his habit of painting variations on a given theme.

Constable's art was a lifelong attempt to render natural scenery more directly and realistically. He was only at home in the country: "The sound of water escaping from mill dams, willows, old rotten planks, slimy posts and brickwork, I love such things. These scenes made me a painter." He set up his easel every day in front of nature, multiplying his sketches from the humblest, simplest, most familiar motifs.

If Constable brought about the triumph of landscape as an independent art form, it was because he, like Leonardo, considered painting as a fundamental science for the investigation of the laws of nature. In one of his lectures at the Royal Institution, in 1833, he declared landscape painting to be both scientific and poetic. It was this attitude that led him to use thick, opaque paints, handled very freely, in his oil sketches. They enabled him to render the mobility of light.

For this purpose Constable progressively developed a palette of more contrasting colours in which the complementaries already appear, despite his attachment to chiaroscuro. An impassioned and searching observer of landscape, of the lights and shadows playing over it, he recorded what he saw with a freshness and accuracy unexampled at that time—so new indeed that he met with persisting incomprehension and was not admitted to the Royal Academy till he was over fifty. His large exhibition pictures were prepared with oil sketches, often in the same format, brushed in quickly in the space of one or two days: he set great store by these working studies from nature, which he kept by him for reference and never sold.

Eugène Delacroix
(1798-1863)
The Entombment, c. 1821.
Oil on canvas.
Copy after Titian's painting
in the Louvre.

Conscious of the disruptions experienced by his generation, Delacroix pondered continually on the meaning and purpose of painting. While he set himself to follow up a new, individual approach to reality, he was always intensely aware of the latter's essential singularity and the necessity of expressing it. Novelty for him lay in "the creating mind and not in painted nature." That same year, 1824, again in his *Journal*, he wrote: "I think that it is imagination alone, or else, what comes to the same, that delicacy of response, which enables one to see what others do not see." Like Turner and Constable, Delacroix felt the need to face nature squarely and scrutinize it, the need to "search into his imagination for the means of rendering nature and effects, and rendering them in accordance with one's own temperament."

Holding aloof from Academy rules and methods, Delacroix looked for models in the museums (then a recent institution), for he felt intensely loyal to the traditions of his art. The Old Masters he copied, however, were only those who appealed to him and stirred his feelings. In this he was followed by all the painters of the nineteenth century, and the effect of this free, individual approach was to diversify the painter's schooling: instead of being tied to a particular studio and master, the young artist ranged widely over the works of the past, choosing to study those that really inspired him. Never were the Old Masters copied so intently as in the nineteenth century; never had their influence on the art of the day been so strong and fruitful.

But to elicit the secrets of the craft, copying was not enough; the "tricks of the trade" were not visible to the naked eye. Delacroix was well aware of this, as his *Journal* shows again and again. He himself was a "dangerous example, leading many artists to tackle their canvas headlong and paint with an ungoverned eagerness, with no thought of the future and no respect for the physical laws of painting technique" (Charles Moreau-Vauthier).

Bitumen was the undoing of much nineteenth-century painting. It was "an unstable colour lending itself readily to every use and every tone, and promptly satisfying any painter who failed to hit on the colour quality of his dark tone" (Moreau-Vauthier). But unless it is thoroughly diluted it never quite solidifies, tearing the oil film and cracking the paint surface. Moreover it creeps about the picture and dirties all the colours. Delacroix's work has suffered much from it; so has that of many nineteenth-century painters.

Though betrayed sometimes by such technical shortcomings, Delacroix stands out nevertheless as one of the boldest experimenters in colour. To step up their brightness, he went so far as to practise a division of tones which makes him a forerunner of the impressionist technique. It can be seen from his *Journal* how much his bold use of colour owed to close observation: "From my window [he was in Dieppe] I see the shadow of people passing in the sun over the sand around the port. The sandy ground here is violet in itself, but made golden by the sun. The shadow of these figures is so violet that the ground becomes yellow." He was so keen an observer of the visible world that he was able to say: "Give me mud and I'll turn it into the skin of a Venus if you leave me free to work it up in my own way."

Continual study of the Old Masters, and chiefly those who went furthest in the development of colour, Rubens, Titian and Veronese, confirmed Delacroix's belief in the still unexplored possibilities of painting. This it was that led him to subordinate details to the whole and kept him on his guard against naturalistic

Eugène Delacroix
(1798-1863)

Combat of the Giaour and
the Pasha Hassan, 1856.
Oil on canvas.

Gustave Courbet
(1819-1877)
The Trellis or Girl
arranging Flowers, 1862.
Oil on canvas.

delineation. Dearer to Delacroix were the more casual-seeming effects of inspiration and spirited handling, so that many of his contemporaries blamed him for what they saw as a failure to finish his work. In fact this lack of finish, this avoidance of "slickness," marks a decisive step forward in the modern autonomy of painting.

Technically speaking, and whatever his assertions to the contrary, Courbet was no innovator. Like Delacroix and even Manet, he remained loyal to the traditions of the past, those of the Dutch and Flemish masters in particular. His investigation of reality, carried out, it is well to remember, in the early days of photography, actually led him to accentuate the painterly effect in order to convey by colour and texture all the insights which the camera failed to record. Courbet was always conscious of the need to individualize his vision and his practice of painting, but he never broke with the habit of studio work, nor with the tradition of beginning the picture on a coloured ground, which has had the effect of darkening

his paintings, for in the end the ground colour shows through. As for open-air painting, it was not till Monet that the picture was done entirely out-of-doors. Courbet kept to his studio, working up his picture piecemeal on the strength of outdoor observation. The result is that his pictures flatter the eye by their wealth of detail but in their entirety fall short of the conviction of visual truth. Hence the disproportion noticeable in the *Trellis*.

Following the great masters of chiaroscuro, Caravaggio and Rembrandt, Courbet worked from dark to light. But to render the tactile and visual perception of things, he employed all the material resources of the painter's craft, not only a variety of brushes but also the sponge and most of all the palette knife. In the same picture, for different effects, he would apply the paints now lightly, now thickly. Above all he stands out as a virtuoso of the palette knife, now increasingly resorted to by painters. With it he massed or spread the pigments to render certain textures and achieved a powerful tactile impression. But by drawing the binder to the surface his thick coats of paint are apt to crack, the drying of the outer layer being much quicker than that of the undercoats which could take years to solidify.

Manet came to the fore in the 1860s just as photography was becoming generalized. The moral and sensual climate which had nourished Courbet's sensibility was by then a thing of the past. Preceding the innovations of photographers, who were still bound by the conventions governing painting, Manet reverted to the "zero degree" of vision. In other words, he effaced himself as completely as possible so that the picture might stand on its own and be seen for its own sake, over and above any preconceived ideas or emotional commitment. In his review of the 1846 Salon (section XVII) Baudelaire wrote: "This glorification of the individual has called for the infinite division of the territory of art... Collective originality has been devoured by individuality, that

little self of one's own... Painting has been killed by the painter." Yet Baudelaire admired the art of Manet, who emphasized the visible as such, untinged by any emotional involvement in it. Brought up in the school of the Northern and the Spanish masters, Manet marks a new departure in technique by his return to the white ground, on which he roughed out his picture as on a drawing board. He aimed at natural light, whose "unity is such that it can be expressed by a single tonality." Till he came under the spell of Impressionism, Manet limited himself to the basic contrast of black and white: it was the foundation of his best pictures. His love of this pure contrast, together with his taste for Japanese prints (which he was one of the first Westerners to admire), led him to simplify the painter's craft, to reconsider the plane of the canvas, to rediscover the sense of the form-defining contour as opposed to contrasting values. Standing back from his subjects,

Edouard Manet
(1832-1883)
The Reading, 1865-1873?
Oil on canvas.

wishing to testify to them without idealizing them, he arrived here at a simplicity of contrasts which, together with his use of back-lighting, enabled him to create a harmony of white unique in the history of painting.

By working exclusively from the motif, out of doors, where he discovered that light is not value but colour, Monet was led to adopt a new manner of painting. The studio manner of the Old

Auguste Renoir
(1841-1919)
Two Bathers, c. 1915.
Oil on canvas.

Masters was of no use to him, intent as he was on recording his optical sensations in broad daylight. For the Old Masters, black and white when identified with light and shade could be mixed progressively with any colour, either directly on the palette or by blending them delicately into the fresh paint on the canvas. But such chemical mixtures are out of the question when a painter finds, as Monet found, that light is orange and shadows blue. To turn a green object, for example, towards orange light by a progressive gradation would result in a transition into dark browns not at all corresponding to the painter's actual perception of nature.

Between 1865 and 1874, date of the first group exhibition of the Impressionists, Monet gained an experience of open-air painting which opened his eyes to visual reality. From his study of sunlight reflected on moving water, he worked out a new system of painting in which each brushstroke stood single and separate, while the picture surface as a whole found its colour harmony by an overall optical fusion. Instead of mixing his colours chemically on the palette, Monet now dotted the canvas with separate strokes of

colour which, by their vibration and interaction, were fused together in the viewer's eye. Without realizing it he was applying Chevreul's theories of simultaneous colour contrasts. By 1874 Monet had mastered this colour-light technique, which was taken over by his fellow Impressionists, by Renoir above all who often worked with him side by side. From then on, painting could no longer be what it had been for the Renaissance masters: a duplication, a window opening on the world, an illusion. By building up the picture in separate strokes of unblended colour, the Impressionists set it up as a reality reconducting the light phenomena which act themselves out in nature. By giving prominence to colour they emphasized its importance as one of the basic components of painting. The latter no longer described nature but recreated it. The oil technique, in itself no longer necessary for this optical divisionism, was then being wholly reconsidered. To work directly from nature, the Impressionists used more opaque, less oily and therefore faster drying paints. To reduce the oil content, they would often spread the colour from the tube over blotting paper, before applying it to the canvas. Like Manet, they adopted

Claude Monet
(1840-1926)
Rouen Cathedral at Dawn,
1894.
Oil on canvas.

a bright ground which gradually showed through and was meant to. They used a more grainy and absorbent canvas which held the paints fast, for with their system there was no reworking the day's picture afterwards: they simply went on to another. Looking on each canvas as a sketch, they reverted to the principle of fat over lean, but gave each brushstroke a roughly identical thickness. Shadows no longer needed to be thinly painted, for they were no longer transparent. They habitually mixed white lead with their pigments, to give them a more mat, more pastel tint. Otherwise the colour as it came from the tube was not much modified, and the rapid execution required to catch fleeting light effects produced that rather dry and scratchy picture surface which only Renoir found uncongenial.

Renoir preferred figure to landscape, though he also liked to combine the two in an easy, gracious fusion. More sensuous, he employed more glazing and varnish than the other Impressionists, till a journey to Italy (1881) led him to revert to a linear style. It was then, in his Ingresque phase, that he moved from a sketchy handling to the smooth paint surface of the Old Masters. But Renoir found no satisfaction in this smooth workmanship, and in his later work he returned to a light, transparent style of painting in which he tended to diminish the whites, for white lead in ageing is apt to absorb all the colours with which it is mixed. In his love of full-blown flesh tints he heightened his pinks. He then developed the procedure which his friend and confidant Albert André describes as follows: "When the subject is simple, he begins his canvas by brushing in, usually in reddish brown, a rough sketch of it... At the second session, when the spirits have rather evaporated, he returns to this preparation, going over it in the same way, but with a mixture of oil and turpentine and a little more colouring matter... He strengthens the shadows and the half-tints, in the same way, directly on the canvas. He does little or no mixing of the tones on the palette, which is covered only with little oily commas of almost pure tones."

Japanese prints had a marked influence on the Impressionists, on Monet in particular. At first

Monet tried out their off-centre composition and their tracts of flat colour, then he attempted to equal their luminosity, which seemed to arise from their flat tones. To do so, he began using less oily paints, over a more absorbent priming, with a medium permitting him to rework without waiting for the paints to dry. This was the period, from the 1880s on, when he was painting variations on the same theme, the Poplars, the Haystacks, the Rouen Cathedrals, the Water Lilies: in these sequences, moving from one canvas to another, he faithfully recorded the changing light, colour and atmosphere of the subject from hour to hour. Here Monet needed to use thick paints, opaque or mat, of a dry enough texture to catch the light impinging on the canvas. To keep this effect unaltered, he gave up varnishing his pictures, a practice that makes them more brilliant but more fragile.

With the Impressionists there occurs a real reversal of painting technique. "Looking at the coats of opaque, rather de-oiled colours of Monet's *Cathedrals* and *Water Lilies*, with their mat and rugged surface (and of other works executed in a similar technique), one begins to wonder, with some alarm, how much now remains of the specific advantages of the oil painting process" (Alexander Ziloty).

Obsessively intent on rendering what he saw in nature, Monet had to admit: "Trying to record weather, atmosphere, surroundings, is enough to drive a man crazy." And again: "The further I go, the more I realize the amount of work involved in rendering what I'm after: the *instantaneousness*, the envelope of things, with the same light pouring in everywhere. More than ever easy canvases done at one go make me sick." Continual reworking was the only way to achieve what he had in mind. "The man who thinks he has finished a canvas is guilty of terrible pride." For Monet, in his researches and experiments, there was no end in sight, as he went on "searching and groping, without achieving much, but wearing myself out in the process." With the all but abstract *Water Lilies* of his last years, he took a decisive step, creating images embodying not a representation of the subject but an idea of it in terms of light and colour.

Claude Monet
(1840-1926)
Rouen Cathedral
in Sunlight, 1894.
Oil on canvas.

Most of the Impressionists and Post-Impressionists used the same technique as Monet, except Gauguin and Van Gogh (and Cézanne for other reasons). Influenced by Japanese prints, and impelled by very definite ideas of their own, Gauguin and Van Gogh took a different view of colour. For them it was not a means of recording light, but a means of expressing their own subjectivity. Colour, for Gauguin, was idea and sentiment; for Van Gogh, emotion and passion. Both aimed at a flat space, but they arrived at it with different techniques because each used it for a different purpose. Gauguin's return to primitivism had direct consequences on his manner of painting, further determined by the fact that, being poor, he had to make shift with cheap materials. In Brittany he began experimenting with unprimed canvas and indeed ordinary sacking (Van Gogh sometimes used it too, after Gauguin's visit to him at Arles in 1888). Jute canvas has an absorbent power which makes the colours more mat, and its coarse grain led Gauguin to reconsider the problem of the outline limiting forms. This was the support he used for his Tahiti pictures, during his two stays there (1891-1893 and 1895-1903), and it sets their character.

The coarse weave of jute or burlap contributes to the primitive look of these pictures. Its grain is everywhere visible, and its absorbent power and natural ochre colour (playing the same harmonic role as the coloured grounds of seventeenth-century painting) fa-voured the muted, internalized tones that he sought. All the more so because Gauguin, an enemy of Western virtuosity, used thin pigments to which he often added wax for increased matness and a regularized surface. Over these broad tracts of flat colour he brushed in subtle modulations. The "supernatural" light that seems to arise from within the picture itself is the direct outcome of these technical features.

Van Gogh, during his Arles period (1888-1889), used pure tones of unexampled thickness. Such profusion was risky and might have been fatal to the preservation of these canvases, but for the soundness of his workmanship, which he owed to his Dutch training. The studio tradition had remained much stronger in Holland than in Paris, and when during his stay in Paris (1886-1888) he initiated himself into Impressionism he did not forget its lessons. His vigorous brushwork, often done in heavy impasto, achieves an ever heightened expressiveness reflecting, by its density and direction, the intensity of his innermost feelings. He instinctively rejected the mat effects of colour which tempted his painter friends, for they would have ruled out the resin he considered essential to his pigments. The resin enveloping them permitted him to contrast complementary colours without their being chemically mixed or altered. Van Gogh's thick and brilliant paints have sometimes cracked with age, but they are sufficiently saturated not to crumble and are protected by a final varnish.

◁ **Paul Gauguin**
(1848-1903)

Whence come we? What are we?
Whither go we?, detail, 1897.
Oil on canvas.

△ **Vincent van Gogh**
(1853-1890)

The Sower, detail,
1888.
Oil on canvas.

83

Paul Cézanne
(1839-1906)

Mont Sainte-Victoire,
detail, 1904-1906.
Oil on canvas.

Painting has a life of its own.
  Jackson Pollock, 1950

6

In his first essay, published in *Art et Critique* (30 August 1890), the young Nabi painter Maurice Denis wrote: "Remember that a picture, before being a war horse, a nude woman or some anecdote, is essentially a flat surface covered with colours arranged in a certain order." Here, summing up Gauguin's ideas, Denis defined the aspiration of the artists of his day. With the Neo-Impressionists, nature imitation ended. The picture was no longer a mirror reflecting an external reality. It became a reality in its own right, as defined by its material components: the canvas or panel, the paints, the forms and colours. This notion underlies all the work of the moderns. It justifies the invention of non-representational art—painting, that is, which communicates simply by what it is. The notion was further extended when "abstract" art was described as "concrete": that is, when the act of painting became the subject of the painting. In this context, technique was shifted onto a new basis: it became the cause and justification of the work.

Paul Klee wrote in 1924: "But what comes up from this plunge into the depths—call it what you will, dream, idea, imagination—cannot really be taken seriously till it has been closely associated with the right plastic means in order to become the Work. Only then do Curiosities become Realities... Because they do not reproduce the visible with more or less of temperament, but make a secret vision visible. With the right plastic means, I said. For it is here that one finds out whether the outcome is a picture or something else." In 1964 the American Frank Stella, who introduced conceptual art, was even more categorical: "My painting is based on the principle that it is only what can be seen that *is* there. It is really an object... What you see is what you see... Nothing more."

As long as painting simulated nature, painting technique appeared as a process of execution. At the beginning of this century, it asserted itself as the place and means of the realization. The point was to produce, not to reproduce. This focus on the actual work of painting may be said to characterize all the experiments of our time, however contradictory they may seem. Seurat, Van Gogh and Gauguin already put the *system and structure* of the picture before representation. So of course did Cézanne, who saw the picture as a "harmony parallel to nature," a specific construction

whose laws had to be discovered. Beginning with the affirmation of the plane defining the canvas, which he often allowed to show through, Cézanne worked out the rhythm of the design and the modulation of the colour in order to achieve the cohesion of a new space. His analytical and critical method, sustained by sheer hard work, had a profound influence. The lack of finish which he allowed himself stands out like a landmark in the history of representation. If the picture is a reality in its own right, the painter has to give due prominence to the terms of his language, the space-plane, line, colour and texture: these are his means of expression. And he makes no secret of his work, its process, evolution, duration and pentimenti being there for all to see. The painting is a living body, a real object.

Marcel Duchamp, a revolutionary artist who gave up painting, laughed at painters as being "doped with turpentine." No matter. Oil painting held its own till the Cubists invented a new technique: collage or assemblage. In 1912, five centuries after Jan van Eyck, the Cubists devised this new technique of pictorial composition which overturned the basics of oil painting. Making much of textural differences, collage offered a syncopated, contrasting medium better attuned to the contemporary sensibility. For the first time the picture was built up with materials other than paints and pigments. Art changed as modern man and modern society changed.

Reality, once the constant source of artistic inspiration, was soon to be left behind in favour of the new media of a new society governed by communication and information. The real no longer lay in the experience of nature but in the photographic print-out of nature. Or more tellingly in painting itself, as painters stood out against the illusionist model of photography and film-making.

But technology continued its advance. Painters were tempted by industrial paints before they began experimenting, in the 1950s, with a new medium offered by modern chemistry: acrylic paints. These combined the resources of watercolour and oils, being quick and easy to apply, without requiring a primed support.

While breaking away from representational art, the twentieth century shifted the focus to the artist's work. The picture became an

Paul Cézanne
(1839-1906)
Mont Sainte-Victoire from
Les Lauves, 1902-1906.
Oil on canvas.

endless experiment and the oil medium gave rise to some moving and unforgettable masterpieces. The present held its own against the past. "The materials I use are paints," said Nicolas de Staël in 1951. "My ideal is determined by my individuality and the individual that I am is made up of all the impressions received from the outside world since my birth and before it."

The Impressionists had tried to record the manifold ways in which light and atmosphere transform natural appearances. Cézanne, though mindful of verisimilitude, went beyond natural appearances. His awareness of the outside world and his way of seeing it were translated into the actual experience of painting, whose components he dissected in his intense search for the truth behind them. The work was no longer meant to communicate by way of memory, but to act on its own. Into the image Cézanne poured the whole charge of his sensations, which he clarified in the act of painting. Representation became inseparable from the making of it.

This rigorous evidencing and questioning of his sensations renewed the artist's relation to both space and time: the latter were no longer external to painting, but integrated into the flow of the painter's emotions. This upsurge and flow is conveyed by the interacting forms, by the brushwork, by the texture of the paints. Cézanne invented a light, transparent technique which permitted him to work in an apparently spontaneous manner, though in fact he spent months on the same picture. He never shrank from letting the bare canvas show through. He never hid the life of the picture, the knifings and scrapings of the paintwork.

Nicolas de Staël
(1914-1955)
Agrigento, 1954.
Oil on canvas.

At the end of a decisive abstract period, in December 1949, Nicolas de Staël asked himself this question: "Can a picture be paintwork and nothing else? I just don't know." From 1951, figures emerge from the close-packed blocks of paint in which the artist pictorially fuses matter, form and colour into an architecture deriving from the land, sea and sky of actual places. Finally, at Le Lavandou on the Riviera, he arrived at pure colour, and in his Sicilian canvases contrasting hues and forms are at their simplest. The object is identified with space, the subject paints the canvas. The long strokes are thinned almost to a wash and the palette knife often takes over. It was better adapted to the modulations and contrasts which give so intense a brightness and vitality to his pictures. For it was only when the colour acts at all points with the same intensity that it rises to its finest glow.

In de Staël's last years one feels him entering the abyss, and with his exploration of it goes an arresting simplicity of form. The paintwork, so dense and pulsing, condenses that multiplicity of effects which nature dissolves in its own mobility and intensity. He was an artist who lived in and through his paintings, each of them arising from the immediacy of personal experience. He saw each

picture as "a force and a feat." "Painting is my way of life, it sets me free from all the impressions, sensations, and qualms that I can only work out through painting." His life experience was channelled into his art.

In his "Notes of a Painter" (1908) Matisse wrote: "Expression, for me, does not lie in the passion that may blaze out in a face or surge up in a violent movement. It is in the whole arrangement of my picture: the place occupied by bodies, the empty spaces around them, the proportions, all this has its share in the expression... In a picture every part will be visible and play its appointed role, a leading one or secondary. Anything that serves no purpose in a picture is thereby harmful. A work of art calls for an overall harmony: any superfluous detail is liable to take up the place of some essential detail in the spectator's mind."

In itself, apart from the intensity of its colours, the oil technique was not indispensable for such expression and harmony. But

Matisse kept to oils up to the late gouache cutouts. Indeed, after Fauvism, he drew fresh resources of invention from it, in his steadily pursued effort to renew the relation between form and colour. "A work of art to be created," he said, "cannot be made in advance... There is no break between the thought and the creative act." Matisse assigned the primary role to colour: "Searching for intensity in colour, texture being immaterial. Reacting against the diffusion of the local tone in light. Light is not done away with, but gets expressed by an attunement of intensely coloured surfaces." This search, proceeding from sensation to idea, to the point of abstraction, led him on to an exemplary economy of means. Starting from the complementaries, he arrived in 1912 at a monochrome scheme which relativized colour and which he later explained: "Feeling is independent of any change of colour. If a green is replaced by a red, the look of the picture may have changed, but not the feeling in it. Colours, I said, are forces. They have to be organized with a view to creating an expressive assemblage."

In the *Red Studio* (1911) Matisse achieved a wonderful complexity with a single colour. By scraping he allowed the undercoats to show through, and they impart further overtones to the red unity. Expressing most with least was his aim.

Haunted by the desire to record features of reality which strike him as ever changing and remote, Alberto Giacometti invented a form of painting which has the suppleness of drawing. In his investigations of a continually fleeting reality glimpsed only through a few focal points which he charted and recharted, always regauging his distances, he resorted to thin, diluted paints which his soft brush traced out with the fineness of pencil strokes. He constantly re-worked his picture, each new lay-in contradicting or redefining the previous record of vision. The painting time with him was long and indeed endless. Like the Old Masters, Giacometti worked from lean to fat, but in the end the thickness of the paints at the main focal points of the image might be no more than a few millimetres. The hand acted in concert with the eye, and the itinerary followed, by way of misgivings and alarms and exultations, is recorded in the paintwork. The pursuit of life is exhausting and inexhaustible. "The distance from one nostril to the other," he said, "is like the Sahara, endless, nowhere to fix the eye, always elusive." In spite of himself Giacometti had to give up colour: "Often in setting to work I've laid out as many colours on my palette as other painters do. I've tried to paint like them. But as

◁ **Henri Matisse**
(1869-1954)
The Red Studio, 1911.
Oil on canvas.

Alberto Giacometti
(1901-1966)
Three Plaster Heads, 1947.
Oil on canvas.

◁ **Pablo Picasso**
(1881-1973)
Violin hanging
on the Wall, 1913.
Oil mixed with sand
on canvas.

▷ **Georges Braque**
(1882-1963)
Soaring Away, 1956-
1961.
Oil on canvas

▽ **André Masson**
(1896)
Lancelot, 1927.
Pasted sand and oil
on canvas.

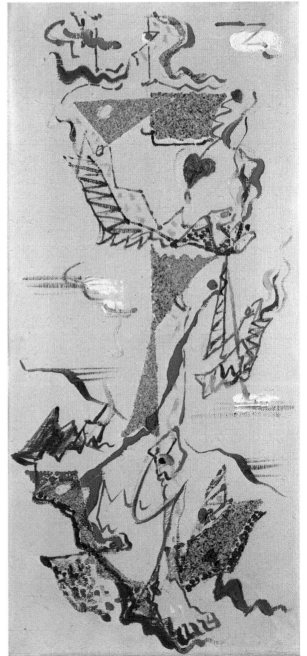

I worked on I eliminated one colour after another. What was left? Grey, grey, grey!'' Painting for Giacometti was a daily attempt to find his bearings in the visible world.

When they invented collage and assemblage in 1912, Braque and Picasso revolutionized the language of modern art. By arranging and pasting all kinds of objects on the painting ground, they broke off the tradition of oil painting based on the unity of space and the imitation of nature. They no longer limited themselves to the classic artist's materials, but made object-pictures with any materials they found to hand in everyday life. They thereby renewed the traditional relation between painting and reality out of which the whole adventure of oil painting had arisen, when it was taken for granted that the picture aimed at recording what the eye saw. Now, instead of painting a musical score or a newspaper, Braque and Picasso simply pasted a score or a strip of newspaper on the canvas, the signifier thus merging with the signified. They thus bridged the gap between reality and its representation.

90

By introducing such materials the Cubists also revolutionized the concept of the picture. Reality no longer lay in an imitation or illusion of it, but in the object of the artist's making. This object, this work, made up now of an assemblage of incongruous materials, was based on discontinuity and contrast, two ever-present features defining the rhythm and sensibility of modern man. And yet Braque and Picasso never gave up oil painting; they even extended its range after their invention of collage.

The son of a house painter, Braque was trained, and thoroughly trained, as a painter decorator: he knew all the tricks of the trade for simulating wood or marble and he passed them on to Picasso. While making the most of assemblage and collage, Picasso did not stop painting. Indeed he extended its power of reality and illusion by availing himself of the decorator's tools, his rakes and toothcombs and brushes, but also by emphasizing the materiality of oils by adding sand and sawdust to them.

When they combine collage with colour, the result is an exhilarating dissociation of line from colour. Tints hitherto had been subordinated to the contour: now these two, each set free of the other, acted as competitors. Colour, all but eliminated in the rigorous Cubism of 1909-1910, accordingly regained its power.

The Surrealist André Masson worked on parallel lines. Marked by Cubism and following up its lead, he relied much on chance effects of paint and line. Letting his brush run free over the canvas, he drew, out of the fruitful tangle of lines, evanescent shapes which he seized on and worked up. In his sand period he sprayed the canvas with glue and scattered sand over it in varying thicknesses and accidental patterns. Masson thus invented a drip technique of his own and exploited it in a whole series of what may be described as automatic paintings. With his sand pictures he gave a new dimension to collage, since here he was painting with actual matter (sand) and by instinct (sense and intensity of his spontaneous gesture).

Still life was a favourite subject with the Cubists because it answered best to their desire to construct their pictures like so many independent objects and set them up as physical realities acting on their own. Why paint a newspaper when you can cut it out and paste it on the canvas? The still life proposed a tactile or manual space as opposed to the visual space of landscape.

Not until he had mastered the tactile realities of still life did Braque move on to landscape, and by then he was beyond nature imitation. For him the picture was a living, material body shaped by the painter's hand: "Writing is not describing, just as painting is not depicting." The infinite no longer lay on the horizon but in the density of the paintwork. Hence the importance of the ground: "I prime my canvases with the utmost care, because the ground is the support on which all the rest stands. It's like the foundations of a house. I've always been occupied and preoccupied by the paints because as much sensibility goes into technique as into the rest of the picture."

For Braque, the spectator had his part to play in the making of the work: "Whoever looks at the canvas follows up the same path as the artist, and since it is the path taken that counts more than the thing, one is more interested by the route."

Soaring Away was begun in 1956 after a journey to Camargue, in the Rhone delta: "The birds inspired me and I tried to make the most of them in my drawings and paintings."

In 1961 Braque took up his picture and reworked it. He complicated his initial image by likening it to his concept, which he added in the lower left corner. The first version had seemed "flawlessly harmonious" but too "habit-ridden": "By adding contradiction and not contention, the whole picture lives now in a more unusual way. These surprise effects are sometimes needed. It keeps you from lapsing into a routine."

While the tricks and recipes of the skilled house painter entered directly into the invention of collage and the development of Synthetic Cubism, these artists were also attracted by the enamel paints which industry was putting on the market for household use. One in particular, Ripolin, patented in 1888, was taken up and continually used by Picasso, beginning as early as 1912.

Another brand used by European painters was Valentine. Both Ripolin and Valentine are industrial oil paints, and laboratory analysts in the museums do not distinguish them from the colours ground for artists. But in fact they are enamel paints whose properties are quite different from those of traditional pigments, and very dissimilar effects can be achieved with them. They are paints moreover which can be mixed in the tin, but they do not lend themselves to fine brushwork. For a flat area of uniform

Francis Picabia
(1879-1953)
The Kiss, c. 1924-1927.
Ripolin on canvas.

Pablo Picasso
(1881-1973)
The Sideboard at Vauvenargues,
1959-1960.
Ripolin on canvas.

colour they are admirable, but not for shading. They dry to a hard, glossy, smooth finish and cannot be painted over. But once collage had been invented and painters had broken away from oils, how could a Picasso or a Pollock resist the urge to work with enamel paints such as any chair or motor car might be painted with? The attraction of these paints lies in their peculiar intensity, and they have the added advantage of being tough and resistant. Picasso used Ripolin in his later cubist compositions, from 1912 on. He gave it up as he entered his neo-classical period towards the close of the First World War, but reverted to it in 1925, beginning with *Three Dancers*, which opened his surrealist period. About the same time the ex-Dadaist Francis Picabia drew violent effects from Ripolin, playing on the cold intensity of its contrasts. Industrial enamel paints favoured expression in terms of flat colour

areas or, on the contrary, could give prominence to line. They could even suggest effects similar to those produced by linocuts. This is what we find in Picasso's *Sideboard at Vauvenargues*, entirely based on the contrast of colour-forms. In his last years Picasso returned often to this type of paint. He appreciated the ease and rapidity of these fluid, quick-drying enamels with their strong covering power. Here the freedom of his brush, the incisiveness of his line, the boldness of his colour schemes, have something in common with the Abstract Expressionists.

Picasso liked the rugged, uneven surface of these paints. They are more alive. They seem to suggest the lapse of time in their creasings and streakings. They lend themselves to direct, telling, primitive expression, to accidental effects and the play of chance. Staying at an inn in Brittany in August 1925, Max Ernst was

Max Ernst
(1891-1976)
The Great Forest, 1927
Oil and grattage
on canvas.

"impressed by the obsession imposed upon my excited gaze by the wooden floor, whose grain had been deepened by countless scrubbings... To aid my meditative and hallucinatory powers, I drop pieces of paper at random on the floor and then rub them with black lead. Examining the drawings thus obtained, I am surprised at the sudden intensification of my visionary faculties." From these rubbings, which he called *frottage*, Ernst went on to devise a pictorial equivalent of it, which he called *grattage*. Covering the canvas with several coats of paint, he placed some objects under it and then scraped off the raised portions of paint, to reveal the under-layers of colour. To this he sometimes added imprints, made with a rag dipped in oil colours. In the *Great Forest* he contrasted the effects of grattage with both transparent and opaque passages of oil paint.

Jackson Pollock
(1912-1956)
Number 3: Tiger, 1949.
Oil and aluminum paint
on canvas mounted on panel.

With the rise of Abstract Expressionism in New York from about 1945 on, the painting became literally the artist's field of action, and so became known as Action Painting. One of its leaders, Willem de Kooning, says: "I'm always somewhere in the picture... I seem to move around in it, until a moment comes when I lose sight of what I wanted to do, and then I'm out of it. If the painting holds its own, I keep it. If not, I get rid of it." To this Jackson Pollock replies: "When I am in my painting, I'm not aware of what I'm doing. It's only after a sort of get-acquainted period that I see what I have been about. I have no fears of making changes, destroying the image, etc., because the painting has a life of its own. I try to let it come through. It is only when I lose contact with the painting that the result is a mess. Otherwise there is pure harmony, an easy give and take, and the painting comes out well."

Pollock played a decisive part in the development of Abstract Expressionism, which took the painting as an unlimited field in which the image arose out of the action of creating an autonomous, real, abstract space as defined by the painter's actual physical exertions. It was only at the end of a long itinerary, by way of Cubism, Picasso and the Surrealists, that Pollock found his distinctive handwriting. By 1947 he had moved on from brushes to the trowel, stick, knife and even his fingers. For the traditional oil pigments he substituted Duco, a high-grade industrial and household paint which flowed freely, and which instead of brushing, he began pouring, throwing and dripping onto his canvas. Action Painting was born. "My painting does not come from the easel... I prefer to tack the unstretched canvas to the hard wall or floor. I need the resistance of a hard surface. On the floor I am more at ease. I feel nearer, more a part of the painting, since this way I can walk around it, work from the four sides and literally be *in* the painting."

Planned design and forethought gave place to instinctive methods akin to automatic writing, the final shapes or patterns being determined by the physical materials and the act of manipulating them. The size of the painting grew: for Pollock, de Kooning and the New York Expressionists there was no set boundary to the canvas, it was an infinite expanse brought to pulsing life by the action of painting, and in the result their work has unprecedented physical vitality.

95

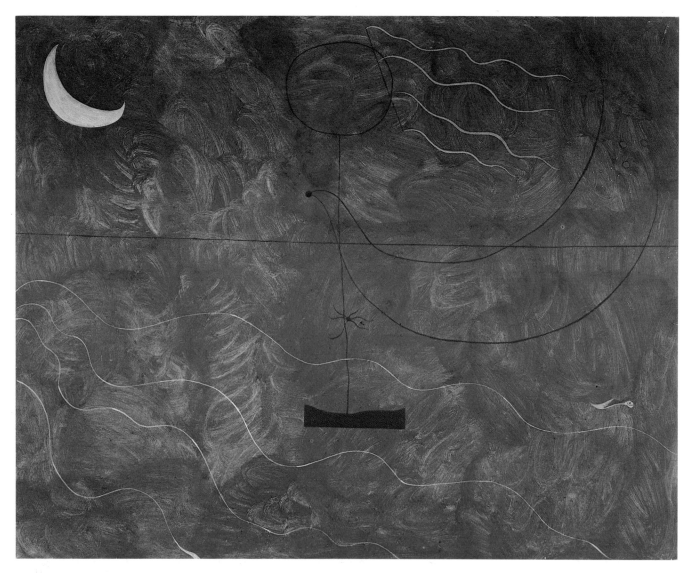

Joan Miró
(1893-1983)
Bather, 1925.
Oil on canvas.

The surrealist painters cannot be described as technical innovators. While they did to some extent renew the traditional practices, their aim rather was to release the primitive forces of the subconscious mind. In the field of collage Max Ernst stands out as a creator of dream images, while Miró and Masson, each with a distinctive originality, created a pictorial equivalent of automatic writing, that "instrument of self-discovery" practised and extolled by André Breton.

The Surrealists saw the image as the vital meeting point between the known and the unknown, the magic place where dreams could be "applied to resolving the fundamental questions of life." For them, the importance of painting lay in its being the very source of revelation.

By 1925 Miró had turned automatic writing into an exclusively pictorial process. This experience brought him to the threshold of abstraction, for it meant a concentration on paintwork and pattern, it meant making ever inventive use of colour, canvas, brushmarks and scrapings to reveal the signwork of biomorphic nature.

The painter gave immediate expression to his inner life, his physical and subconscious self. By doing so, he reversed the hierarchy of values connected with traditional technique in which the image started out from the drawing. Miró, on the contrary, started out from the void, gradually filling it up from his own resources of fancy and imagination: "Instead of taking something to paint, I simply start painting, and as I paint, the picture begins to take shape under my brush or give intimations of itself. The form becomes a sign of woman or bird as I go on with the work. The first stage is free and unconscious."

Rothko has a different conception of the painter's work: "The picture has to be a miracle. The moment it is finished, the intimacy between the creation and the creator is broken off. It is a stranger." For him as for Pollock, painting is a necessity: "I believe that being abstract or figurative is not the question. The thing to do is put an end to this silence and solitude, to breathe and stretch our arms again." But the space that he develops in his painting is the very opposite of that of the Expressionists.

96

Mark Rothko
(1903-1970)
Red, White and Brown, 1957.
Oil on canvas.

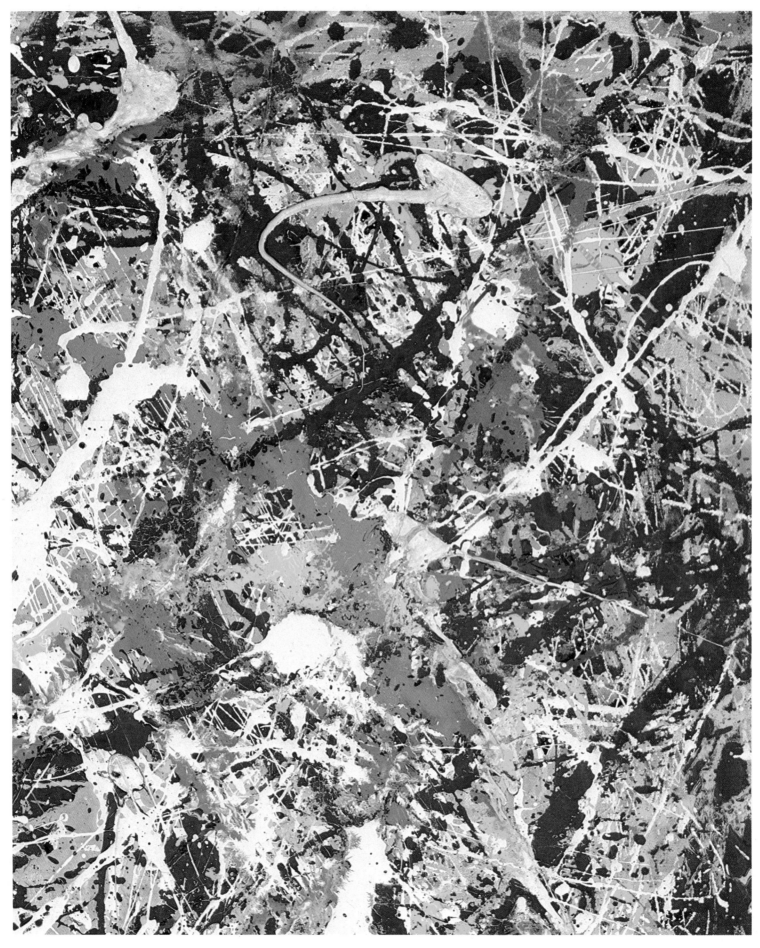

Rothko aims at depth. His experience as a decorator and above all as a watercolourist taught him to use the support and exploit its absorbent power. Over unprimed cotton canvases he spread very thin coats of colour which penetrated in depth more than they covered. Thinned with turpentine and made translucent, his colour soaks in and gains its intensity from repeated overlayers: one cannot foresee or describe in advance the action or the pictorial agents. "It all begins like an unknown adventure in an unknown place. It is only at the finish, in a flash of awareness, that their expected quantity and function are recognized. The ideas and plans one had in mind at the start were only a passage through which one left the world they welled up from."

Very spiritualistic, Rothko grouped his canvases in sets, and so heightened the effect he meant to get from their large size. "I paint large canvases," he said, "because I want to create a state of intimacy. A large painting implies an immediate exchange. It takes you with it."

Soaking into the canvas surface like a dye: such was the very power of the new acrylic technique, and in his last works Rothko switched over to it from oils.

When acrylic paints appeared on the market in the 1950s, it looked as if oil painting had had its day, after a run of five centuries. Acrylics seemed destined to supersede oils because better adapted to today's requirements. They do not deteriorate, they dry very quickly, they can be worked over with no particular precautions and can be applied without priming to any support.

Used at first for industrial purposes, acrylic paints were noticed and taken up by a whole group of American painters as answering their need for ready-made paints which penetrate the raw support, show the brushmark well, favour the chance play of strokes and streakings, and lend themselves to flat colour areas without ruling out mixing. By the late 1970s even the most conservative painters were making use of them. But it was soon realized that they are harder and drier than oil paints, and that they do not have the same luminous depth or comparable tactile effects. Moreover, since the 1980s, in the wake of the trans avant-garde and neo-expressionism, oil painting has made a comeback. Italian, German and even French and American artists are reverting to the old oil technique, re-exploring its wonderful possibilities and at the same time multiplying quotations from earlier masters. Is this a renaissance or the climax of a dazzling display of fireworks? It would be rash to give a definite answer, at a time when anything seems possible, even in painting.

This much may be said. The twentieth century has upset and interrupted the evolution of oil painting by the invention of collage and the introduction of acrylics. Collage revolutionized the very language of art. Acrylics renewed the practice of art by opening up other possibilities. This happened at a time when the creative artist was less intent on working out a specific style or manner than on finding, for each situation, a suitable technical response. Which is to say, in effect, that technique in itself has less importance today than in the past. Our civilization has also become aware of the fact that reality, both in the big and the small, far outstrips the seeing power of the eye, and oil painting was created for the purpose of reducing the visible world to the scale of man, of bringing nature into the range of sight. The crisis of oil painting, whether surmountable or not, remains: a tradition of five centuries' standing has been challenged. The outcome lies in the future. Confidence in its future seems justified when one surveys the history of a technique which, from the fifteenth century to today, has permitted the creation of so many masterpieces.

Jackson Pollock
(1912-1956)
Number 3: Tiger,
detail, 1949.
Oil and aluminum paint
on canvas mounted on panel.

How oil colours are made

Composition of an oil colour:
pigment
oil
extender (according to the pigment)
drier (according to the type of pigment)

Manufacture
This is done in two stages:

Impasting: the different ingredients are mixed in a vat with revolving blades.
When well mixed, the grains of pigment are still too big for the use of painters. They must be finely ground: this is the second stage.

Grinding: in a three-roller mill, the pigment is dispersed in the liquid vehicle so that each particle of pigment is well coated with oil. After an initial grinding, the degree of fineness is checked; then the pigment is ground once again before the batch of colour is poured off into pots.
Two grindings are usually enough, but three or four may be necessary for particularly hard pigments.
The grinding mill is equipped with rollers of case-hardened steel; for particularly brittle pigments, with granite rollers working more slowly and less roughly than the steel ones.
The fineness of the grinding is measured by the North gauge and varies from 8.5 to 9.
The ground colour is stocked for a month or two in pots; after being checked again, it is poured off into tubes.
Today the grinding of colours is a perfectly ordinary operation, presenting no particular difficulty. What is more delicate is the choice of ingredients for each colour: on their choice and condition depends the quality of the final product.

Checking the ingredients

The pigments have to be tested for their freshness of tone, ease of grinding, permanence and stability in light.

Each new pigment is ground, then applied to canvas, and after drying exposed for two years, facing south, behind a glass pane, part of the pigment being screened from the light. After two years, the two parts, one exposed, one screened, are compared, and from the results we determine the number of stars denoting stability in light.

At the same time we carry out an accelerated ageing test: 344 hours' exposure to infrared and ultraviolet rays, corresponding to four years' exposure in sunlight.

Comparison of these two tests gives the final classification of the pigment.

The oil is chosen on the basis of its acidity and its resistance to yellowing—standards which, at the present time, can be met by any reliable supplier.

The extender is chosen for its colourlessness when ground in oil, and for its inertia—that is, its failure to weaken the tinting strength of the pigment.

The drier, added in small amounts determined by testing, accelerates the drying of an oil paint. For some pigments containing a native siccative element, it is not needed.

An important point to remember is that, if too large an amount is added, the drier has the opposite effect: the paints fail to dry, causing accidents as the picture ages.

Colour tubes carry important information on the label:

The stars indicate the degree of stability in light:

3 ✶✶✶ – a colour permanent in full tone and shadings.
2 ✶✶ – permanent in full tone but less stable in shadings.
1 ✶ – less stable in full tone and in shadings.
No star means that there is no guarantee of stability over a period of time.

The chemical nature of the pigment constituting the colour shade.

The letter M means that the colour can be mixed in any proportion with any other colour shade.

The absence of the letter M means that it is risky to mix this colour with any other also having no letter M on the tube label. An example of two unmixables: chrome yellow (lead chromate) + cadmium red (sulfoselenium of cadmium); the presence of sulphur with lead may in time cause darkening.

But a colour marked M can be mixed without risk with any colour not marked with M.

Jean Riccarand
Head of the Laboratory
Firm of Lefranc & Bourgeois
Paris, March 1985

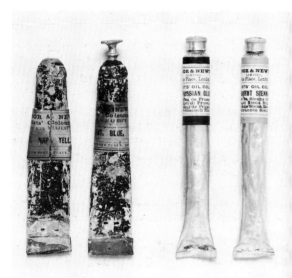

Artists' colourmen in London supplied ready-made oil colours as far back as the early seventeenth century, and, after that time, both manufacturers and artists had to contend with the problem of a suitable container. It had to be sufficiently airtight to keep the oil colours from oxidizing and hardening, and, in addition, it had to be sufficiently adaptable for a painter to extract some colour and preserve the rest for a future occasion.

Until the early nineteenth century, skin bladders were the customary containers, each bag being drawn together at the top and tightly bound so that air was excluded. When a painter wanted to extract some colour he punctured the bladder with a tack, squeezed out the paint and then stopped up the hole with the tack or a plug of ivory or bone. Bladders had a number of disadvantages. They sometimes burst when squeezed. Although most colours kept fairly well in unperforated bladders, Prussian blue and red lakes were reputed to deteriorate, and all began to oxidize once the skin was punctured. It is surprising that bladders should have been used for so long, but by the nineteenth century an ever-growing number of amateurs probably increased the need for alternative containers. James Harris submitted "a syringe for the purpose of preserving oil paint" to the Society of Arts, London, in April 1822. It was made of brass tinned on the inside. Through a nozzle at one end the colour could be pushed out; a small cap was screwed on when the syringe was not in use. The other end was fitted with a large screw cap which was also threaded for the screw to pass through it. The cap could be removed so that the piston, made of cork covered with leather, could be pulled right out to enable the cylinder to be filled with colour.

For a brief period glass syringes were also available. They were patented in 1840 by William Winsor who, eight years previously, had established an artists' colour business, in partnership with H. C. Newton.

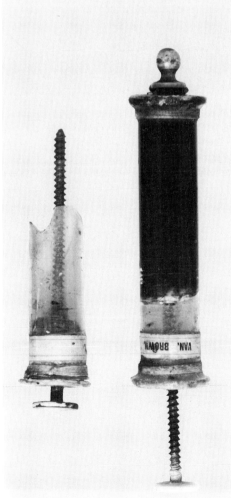

In January 1841 Waring and Dimes, colourmen in London, advertised their "Anti-tube bladders of oil colour," that is, traditional bladders fitted with a cap which, when removed, allowed paint to be squeezed out through the neck.

The invention that was to have the greatest impact was announced in June 1841: collapsible colour tubes. The inventor was John G. Rand, an American portrait painter then resident in London. Winsor and Newton set out to make their own tubes, formed of thin rolls or layers of metal, the interior lined with a membrane to isolate pigment from the metal; each tube was fitted with a stopper. In the art world collapsible tubes were adopted immediately and they made outdoor painting easier for nineteenth-century artists.

R. D. Harley
Technical Liaison Officer
Winsor and Newton Ltd.
Wealdstone, Harrow, England.
Abridged from "Oil colour containers:
development work by artists and
colourmen in the nineteenth century"
in Annals of Science, *March 1971.*

Photographs of colour bladders, syringes
and tubes by courtesy of
Winsor and Newton Ltd.

Eugène Delacroix (1798-1863): Liberty Leading the People
(28 July 1830), 1830. Oil on canvas. (8 ft. 6 in. ×
10 ft. 8 in.)
Musée du Louvre, Paris.

Delacroix's
"Liberty Leading
the People"
studied in the
research laboratory
of the French National
Museums, Paris

by Lola Faillant-Dumas
and Jean-Paul Rioux

"I have undertaken a modern subject, a barricade... If I did not fight for our country, at least I will paint for it," wrote Delacroix to his brother in October 1830, and his large picture was finished before the end of the year. Was it painted at one go? Does the composition betray any hesitations and changes? Certainly many preparatory studies were made, chiefly for the figure of Liberty, but they do not precisely correspond to the final picture. The laboratory examination was made in an attempt to trace the different stages of its making.

X-ray examination

Today the X-ray study of a painting is common practice and can add considerably to our knowledge of a work. Any investigation into Delacroix's methods in painting his *Liberty* must begin here.

The image obtained by X-rays accentuates the contrast of shadows and lights and brings out the fantastic aspect of the scene: the pyramidal design emphasized at the top by the density of the whites building up the stalwart figure of the woman; at the bottom the cold, forthright lights glowing on the dead figures in the foreground.

The canvas is of a somewhat coarse and irregular weave, with fourteen warp and eleven woof threads per square centimetre.

The main interest of the X-ray lies in showing the revision made in the figure of Liberty. Initially, her face was painted almost in front view, looking downward. Her ample robe flared out to the left, emphasizing her powerful stride. The shoulder to the right was barer, and the broad sleeve came down over the arm, itself extended along the body. This attitude corresponds more closely to the preparatory drawings preserved in the Cabinet des Dessins of the Louvre. But Delacroix proceeded to modify it, turning the face away in side view, cleaving the ample robe to her body, raising the top of it to her left shoulder, bending her arm and adjusting the rifle. Liberty was thus immobilized in her present position, with her eyes fixed on the man with a top hat. And the size of the flag was reduced.

What about the street urchin beside her? He was moved slightly to the right, as shown by the changes made in the contours of his jacket and arms.

With these hesitations behind him, Delacroix repainted the colour in the area between the woman and the boy, to set them distinctly apart.

On either side of these two figures, the background has no secrets to reveal. The paints are thinly applied. A few white accents set off the houses on the right (the roofs being lowered in the final execution) or convey the metallic lustre of the weapons on the left. The crowd on the left remains largely undefined; here Delacroix made no changes in the course of his work.

The foreground figures were broadly and rapidly brushed in, with pure whites for shirt, gaiters and Swiss guard uniform, to reinforce the brutal reality of the scene. The extreme edges of the composition, to right and left, are less thickly painted than the central area, and some details (left arm of the man with a sword on the left, the tangle of wooden posts and planks on the right) remain imprecise. The lack of definition here is apparently due not to any reworking in 1830 but rather to subsequent retouching made when the picture was exhibited in 1848 and 1855, after some years in poor conditions of conservation. This would explain the excessive darks on and behind the right arm of the man in a top hat, and also along the lower edge of the canvas.

It may be too that, for so big a picture, Delacroix was economizing his colours in the secondary parts, concentrating them on the central scene—symbol of a momentous contemporary event. For the background areas are lightly brushed in with, however, some working out of nuances with a view to that colour harmony which Delacroix achieved so delicately in his mixtures.

The X-ray shows the painter's brushwork and craftsmanship. Flesh tints are modelled in a dark scale, with a broad, flexible brush, according to Delacroix's usual technique in his large figure compositions—a technique which he describes several times in his *Journal* and which laboratory analysis has already revealed in other pictures of his. The brushstrokes are astonishingly rapid; they show a masterly handling of broad colour areas in full light, and in the figure of Liberty they go to emphasize her strenuous forward stride and turning movement.

This initial examination makes it clear that we are in the presence of a picture partially reworked by the artist. It remains for the stratigraphic study of the paint layers to specify the different stages of these changes and to define the characteristics of the paintwork. The disposition and internal structure of the different paint layers can be determined by microscopic observation of minute samples of them. Chemical analysis of these samples goes to complete the study by identifying the ingredients of the paints.

Examination of the paint layers

Several samples of paint, of different colours, have been taken from the picture and examined. Comparison of them shows first of all that the priming coat is not uniform over the canvas as a whole. Its very light-hued buff colour varies from place to place either towards pale grey or a deeper-hued buff. White lead and oil are the main ingredients of this priming coat.

On this light-hued ground, the rough sketch was brushed in with a brown paint rich in a binding medium containing oil and resins. This sketch did no more than rough out the volumes and design. From this point the main colours were indicated, and parts in the light were heightened with a bright grey and bright buff. This sketch therefore represented a relatively advanced stage of the picture. From what we know of Delacroix's great skill, we may assume that it was built up very quickly.

The paints are variously worked from place to place. At some points they simply consist of one thick coat designed to give body to the underlying sketch; sometimes a thin over-layer is added to define relief or draping. This is the case, for example, with the flag and the jacket of the man at the feet of Liberty looking up at her.

The stratigraphy of the darker colours is equally simple. They are treated in thick brown glazes partially opaque and shaded by the addition of ground dark pigments. The brighter colours, however, often have a more complex structure, several coats being superimposed, so that the hue gradually changes. This does not mean that he was seeking a special effect from a sequence of various coats, for these, rich in white lead, are individually quite opaque. What it means rather is that the final surface color is the result of the painter's sustained search for the right colour and his effort to harmonize it with the rest of the composition. So it is that the subtlest of the brighter colours, like the robe of Liberty or the smoke cloud behind her, are seen to be carefully worked over; unlike the ground sketch and the darker colours, they are the fruit of a slower, less spontaneous elaboration.

The colours identified by chemical analysis form a restricted palette. Apart from white lead, the commonest pigment here is a brown earth colour of the *terre de Cassel* type, used for the purpose of deepening the darker colours or shading the greys and buffs. The yellow, painted chiefly as an over-layer, was not made with an opaque pigment but with a lake either mixed with white to obtain a pale yellow or applied as a transparent glazing. This technique was used chiefly for finishing the garments of Liberty. Also present are some pigments modern for the period, such as cobalt blue which was invented in the early nineteenth century. All the colours number among those habitually used by Delacroix, as we know from the orders he sent to Haro, his colourman in Paris.

Pentimenti and overpaintings are detected and localized initially by X-ray examination. Stratigraphic study of the paint layers in these places goes to complete the initial findings by giving us further information about the underpainting before modification.

So it is that comparison of the stratified coats of paint in the robe of Liberty and in the smoke cloud immediately to the right of her hip shows the presence of identical undercoats corresponding to the initial, ampler version of her robe. The latter, of a bright yellow fairly close to that of the final version, had been carried beyond the state of the initial rough sketch when Delacroix returned to it and entirely repainted the whole robe.

The Phrygian cap shows another example of overpainting. Its deep reddish colour is the result of five successive coats of paint. This complex stratigraphy vouches for Delacroix's hesitation in choosing the colour. An initial bright red was toned down with an initial reddish buff glazing, then with a second purplish blue glazing. Next came two coats of orange and a further glazing.

Examination of a paint sample from the smoke cloud to the left of the houses shows that the surface colour was laid over a pale, faintly bluish grey. The suggestion put forward, that there may have been a landscape in this part of the picture, belonging to an initial, different, unfinished composition, is not necessarily refuted by the examination of this one paint sample. The suggestion does, however, fail to carry conviction in view of the fact that neither X-rays nor paint samples from all over the picture have revealed any compositional elements notably different from the composition as we see it now.

The results obtained illustrate the usefulness of X-ray examination combined with stratigraphic analysis of the paints, as a complement to the study of documents relating to the history of the picture. These scientific techniques provide a source of further knowledge about Delacroix's manner of painting and offer fresh insights into the working of his creative mind.

This study is part of Dossier No. 26
of the Department of Paintings, Musée du Louvre:
La Liberté guidant le peuple de Delacroix,
Editions de la Réunion des Musées Nationaux,
Paris, 1982.

▷ *Full-size X-ray photograph of the head of Liberty in Delacroix's* Liberty Leading the People, *1830. Photograph by courtesy of the Laboratoire de Recherche des Musées de France, Paris.*

The Paris firm of Gustave Sennelier, manufacturer of fine colours and artists' materials, was founded in 1873. It is still in business. Among its early customers were the Impressionists and in particular Cézanne, who often came to the shop.

A life class in the Colarossi art school, Paris.
Photograph by Clive Holland, from The Studio,
London, 15 October 1902.

Studio easels on rollers, from Gustave
Sennelier's 1895 catalogue.

Corot painting at Saint-Nicolas,
near Arras, July 1873.
Photograph by Charles Desavary.
The purpose of the sunshade
was to shield the canvas from
sunlight and so keep the
paints from drying too quickly.

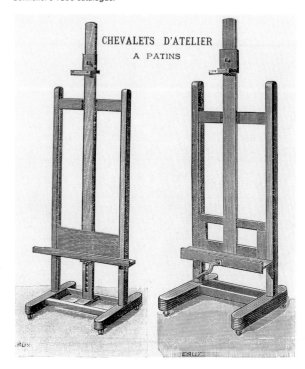

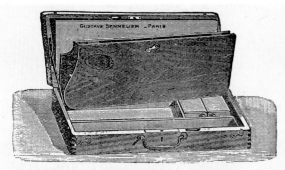

BOITE ÉTROITE, PALETTE PLIANTE

Paint box with folding palette, colour tubes, artists' sunshades, palette knife and landscape easels, from Gustave Sennelier's 1895 catalogue.

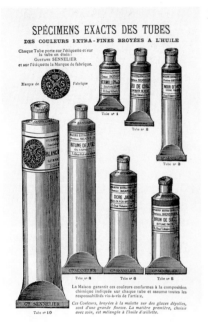

CHEVALETS DE CAMPAGNE

Chevalet à coulisses   Chevalet belge

COUTEAUX A PALETTES
en acier anglais extra-fin, manche coco

Lame droite

Cézanne painting at Aix-en-Provence, January 1904. Photograph taken by Maurice Denis accompanied by Emile Bernard.

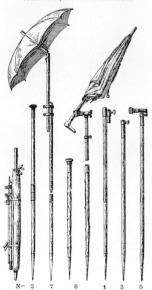

PARASOLS D'ARTISTES
TOILE GRISE, MONTURE ACIER CREUX

Johann Zoffany (1734/35-1810): The Tribune of
the Uffizi in Florence with English Art Lovers,
*1780. Oil on canvas. Windsor Castle, reproduced
by gracious permission of Her Majesty The Queen.*

*A man doesn't say "I'll be a painter" in front of
a beauty spot, but in front of a picture.*

Auguste Renoir

Bibliography

List of Illustrations

Index of Names

Bibliography

A selective listing, with some English translations, of general works on the technique and theories of painting which were used and consulted in the writing of this book.

Leon Battista ALBERTI, *De pictura*, 1435 (Italian version, *Della pittura*, 1436); first printed, Basel, 1540; edited by Malle, Florence, 1951; English translation by John R. Spencer, New Haven and Oxford, 1956. — E.E. AMAURY-DUVAL, *L'atelier d'Ingres*, Paris, 1878. — Louis ARAGON, *La peinture au défi*, Paris, 1930; *Les collages*, Paris, 1965. — Pietro ARETINO, *Lettere*, 6 vols., Paris, 1609; new edition, *Lettere sull'arte*, 4 vols., Milan, 1957-1960.

Edgard BAES, *Recherches sur les couleurs employées par les peintres depuis l'antiquité jusqu'à nos jours*, Brussels, 1883. — Filippo BALDINUCCI, *Notizie de' professori del disegno da Cimabue in qua*, 6 vols., Florence, 1681-1728; included in *Opere*, 11 vols., Milan, 1811-1812; reprinted in 7 vols., Florence, 1974-1975; *Vocabolario toscano dell'arte del disegno*, Florence, 1681. — P. BAROCCHI, *Trattati d'arte del Cinquecento fra Manierismo e Controriforma*, 3 vols., Bari, 1960-1962. — G.P. BELLORI, *Le vite de' pittori scultori ed architetti moderni*, Rome, 1672; 3rd edition, Pisa, 1821; reprinted Rome, 1931; *Vite di Guido Reni, Andrea Sacchi e Carlo Maratti*, edited by Michelangelo Piacentini, Rome, 1942. — Ernst BERGER, *Beiträge zur Entwickelungs-Geschichte der Maltechnik*, 5 vols., Munich, 1897-1909: *Quellen und Technik der Fresko-, Öl- und Tempera-Malerei des Mittelalters*, 3rd volume, and *Quellen für Maltechnik während der Renaissance und deren Folgezeit in Italien, Spanien, den Niederlanden, Deutschland, Frankreich und England*, 4th volume. — Charles BLANC, *Grammaire des arts du dessin. La peinture*, Paris, 1885 ff. — Marco BOSCHINI, *La carta del navegar pitoresco*, Venice, 1660; *Le ricche minere della pittura veneziana*, Venice, 1664, 2nd enlarged edition, Venice 1672. — Abraham BOSSE, *Le peintre converty aux précises et universelles règles de son art*, Paris, 1677; edited by R.A. Weigert, Paris, 1964. — Cesare BRANDI, *Teoria del restauro*, Rome, 1963. — E.W. BRÜCKE, *Die Physiologie der Farben für die Zwecke der Kunstgewerbe*, Leipzig, 1866; French translation, *Des couleurs au point de vue physique, physiologique, artistique et industriel*, Paris, 1866. — Maurice BUSSET, *La technique moderne du tableau et les procédés secrets des grands coloristes des XVᵉ, XVIᵉ et XVIIᵉ siècles*, Paris, 1929.

Ettore CAMESASCA, *Artisti in bottega*, Milan, 1966. — A.C.P. de CAYLUS, *Nouveaux sujets de peinture et sculpture*, Paris, 1755. — Cennino CENNINI, *Il libro dell'arte*, c. 1400, first published by Tambroni, Rome, 1821; edited by Gaetano Milanesi, Florence, 1859; English version, *The Craftsman's Handbook*, translated by Daniel V. Thompson, Jr., New Haven and London, 1933; reprinted, New York, 1954 and 1961. — M.E. CHEVREUL, *Recherches expérimentales sur la peinture à l'huile*, Paris, 1850. — C.N. COCHIN, *Recueil de* quelques pièces concernant les arts, Paris, 1757. – W.G. CONSTABLE, *The Painter's Workshop*, London and New York, 1964.

Pierre DAIX, *Cubists and Cubism*, Geneva, London, New York, 1982. – Charles DALBON, *Les origines de la peinture à l'huile*, Paris, 1904. – H. DAMISCH, *Fenêtre jaune cadmium ou les dessous de la peinture*, Paris, 1984. – Eugène DELA-CROIX, *Journal*, edited by André Joubin, 3 vol., Paris, 1932, 1950, 1980; *Correspondance*, edited by André Joubin, 5 vols., Paris, 1935-1938. – Maurice DENIS, *Théories (1890-1910)*, Paris, 1912, 1920. – J.B. DESCAMPS, *La vie des peintres flamands, allemands et hollandais*, 4 vol., Paris, 1753-1764. – Denis DIDEROT, *Essai sur la peinture* and *Sur l'origine et la nature du beau*, in *Œuvres complètes*, 15 vols., Paris, 1798, 1951; *Salons, 1759-1781*, edited by Jean Seznec and Jean Adhémar, Oxford, 1957 ff.; *Sur l'art et les artistes*, edited by Jean Seznec, Paris, 1967. – Etienne DINET, *Les fléaux de la peinture*, Paris, 1926. – Lodovico DOLCE, *Dialogo della pittura intitolato "L'Aretino,"* Venice, 1557; reprinted in P. Barocchi, *Trattati d'arte*, Bari, 1960-1962. – Bernardo De DOMINICI, *Vite de' pittori, scultori, ed architetti napoletani*, 3 vols., Naples, 1742-1744. – DOS-SIERS DU DÉPARTEMENT DES PEINTURES DU MUSÉE DU LOUVRE: *Technique de la peinture, l'atelier*, by J. Baticle, P. Georgel, N. Willk-Brocard, Paris, 1976; *Restauration des peintures*, by S. Bergeon, G. Emile-Mâle, L. Faillant-Dumas, Paris, 1980; *Conservation et restauration, peintures des musées de Dijon*, by S. Bergeon, P. Georgel, Paris, 1983. – Abbé J.B. DUBOS, *Réflexions critiques sur la poésie et la peinture*, Paris, 1719. – Albrecht DÜRER, *Hierin sind begriffen vier Bücher von menschlicher Proportion*, Nuremberg, 1528; cf. K. Lange and F. Fuhse, *Albrecht Dürers schriftlicher Nachlass*, Halle, 1893.

Sir Charles EASTLAKE, *Materials for a History of Oil Painting*, 2 vols., London, 1847-1869; reprinted as *Methods and Materials of Painting of the Great Schools and Masters*, 2 vols., New York and London, 1960. – G. EMILE-MÂLE, *Restauration des peintures de chevalet*, Fribourg (Switzerland), 1976; *The Restorer's Handbook of Easel Painting*, New York, 1976. – ERACLIUS, *De coloribus et artibus romanorum*, published in R.E. Raspe, *A Critical Essay on Oil Painting*, London, 1781, and in Mary P. Merrifield, *Original Treatises*, London, 1849.

André FÉLIBIEN, *De l'origine de la peinture*, Paris, 1660; *Entretiens sur la vie et les ouvrages de Nicolas Poussin*, Geneva, 1947. – LA FONT DE SAINT-YENNE, *Réflexions sur la peinture*, Paris, 1746; *Réflexions sur quelque cause de l'état présent de la peinture en France*, The Hague, 1747. –

R. FRÉART DE CHAMBRAY, *Idée de la perfection de la peinture*, Le Mans, 1662. – Eugène FROMENTIN, *Les maîtres d'autrefois*, 1876; edited by J. Foucart, Paris, 1965; *The Masters of Past Time, Dutch and Flemish Painting from Van Eyck to Rembrandt*, translated by Andrew Boyle, edited by H. Gerson, London and New York, 1948.

Thomas GAINSBOROUGH, *Letters*, edited by M. Woodall, London and Greenwich, Conn., 1963. – R.J. GETTENS and G.L. STOUT, *Painting Materials, A Short Encyclopedia*, New York, 1942. – Lorenzo GHIBERTI, *I commentarii*, first published from the manuscript in the Biblioteca Nazionale, Florence, by Julius von Schlosser in *Lorenzo Ghiberti's Denkwürdigkeiten*, Berlin, 1912; edited by O. Morisani, Naples, 1947; *Il secondo commentario*, edited by G. Niccolai, Florence, 1956. – J.G. GOULINAT, *La technique des peintres*, Paris, 1926. – Don Felipe de GUEVARA, *Commentarios de la pintura*, Madrid, 1788, and Barcelona, 1948.

Marc HAVEL, *La technique du tableau*, Paris, 1974. – Francisco de HOLLANDA, *Tractato de pintura antigua*, 1548; Oporto, 1896; edited by Pelizzari, Naples, 1914; *Four Dialogues on Painting*, translated by A.F.G. Bell, Oxford, 1928. – M. HOURS, *Analyse scientifique de conservation des peintures*, Fribourg (Switzerland), 1976.

Gerard de LAIRESSE, *Het groot Schilderboeck*, Amsterdam, 1707; *The Art of Painting*, translated by J.F. Fritsch, London, 1738, 1778 and 1817. – A.P. LAURIE, *The Pigments and Mediums of the Old Masters*, London, 1914; *The Painter's Methods and Materials*, Philadelphia and London, 1926, and London, 1947. – LEONARDO DA VINCI, *Trattato della pittura*, 1490-1519; Paris, 1650, 1651; Bologna, 1786; *Treatise on Painting*, Italian text with English translation by A. Philip McMahon, 2 vols., Princeton, 1956. – G.E. LESSING, *Laokoon oder Über die Grenzen der Malerei und Poesie*, Berlin, 1776; *Laocoön*, translated by W.A. Steel, London, 1930; *Vom Alter der Ölmalerei aus dem Theophilus Presbyter*, Braunschweig, 1774. – André LHOTE, *Les invariants plastiques*, edited by Jean Cassou, Paris, 1967. – G.P. LOMAZZO, *Trattato dell'arte della pittura, scoltura et architettura*, Milan, 1584; *Idea del Tempio della pittura*, Milan, 1590; reprinted Rome, 1947. – G. LOUMYER, *Les traditions techniques de la peinture médiévale*, Brussels and Paris, 1914.

R.H. MARIJNISSON, *Dégradation, conservation et restauration de l'œuvre d'art*, Brussels, 1967. – J.F.L. MÉRIMÉE, *De la peinture à l'huile ou Des procédés matériels employés dans ce genre de peinture depuis Hubert et Jan van Eyck jusqu'à nos jours*, Paris, 1830; *The Art of Painting in Oil*, London, 1839. — Mary P. MERRIFIELD, *Original Treatises, Dating from the XIIth to XVIIIth Centuries on the Arts of Painting*, 2 vols., London, 1849; reprinted, 2 vols., New York and London, 1967. — MICHELANGELO BUONARROTI, *Lettere*, edited by G. Milanesi, Florence, 1875; *Le rime*, edited by C. Guasti, Florence, 1863; *Sonnets*, translated by J.A. Symonds, London and New York, 1904. — Charles MOREAU-VAUTHIER, *La Peinture*, Paris, 1913, 1933; *The Technique of Painting*, London and New York, 1917; *Comment on peint aujourd'hui*, Paris, 1923. — Lewis MUMFORD, *Art and Technics*, New York, 1950.

Francisco PACHECO, *Arte de la pintura, su antiguedad y grandezas*, Seville, 1649, and Madrid, 1866. — G.B. PASSERI, *Vite de'pittori, scultori ed architetti che hanno lavorato in Roma, morti dal 1641 fino al 1673*, Rome, 1772, and Vienna, 1934. — Jean PÉLERIN, see VIATOR. — A. PELLIZZARI, *I trattati attorno le arti figurative in Italia e nella Penisola Iberica: Vol. I, Dall'antichità classica al secolo XIII*, Naples, 1915; Vol. II, *Dal secolo XIII al XVI*, Genoa, Rome, Naples, 1942. — Roger de PILES, *Abrégé de la vie des peintres*, Paris, 1699; in English, London, 1706 and 1744; *Eléments de peinture pratique*, Paris, 1684-1685; *Cours de peinture par principes*, Paris, 1708; in English, London, 1743. — PIERO DELLA FRANCESCA, *Petrus Pictor Burgensis, De prospectiva pingendi*, 1482, first published Strasbourg, 1899; critical edition by G.N. Fasola, Florence, 1974. — Paolo PINO, *Dialogo di pittura*, Venice, 1548; reprinted in P. Barocchi, *Trattati d'arte*, Bari, 1960-1962. — Nicolas POUSSIN, *Lettres*, edited by Pierre du Colombier, Paris, 1929; *Lettres et propos sur l'art*, edited by Anthony Blunt, Paris, 1964.

Sir Joshua REYNOLDS, *Fifteen Discourses delivered in the Royal Academy*, Everyman's Library, London and New York, 1907; *Discourses on Art*, edited by R.R. Wark, San Marino (California), 1959. — Jonathan RICHARDSON, *An Essay on the Theory of Painting*, London, 1715; *The Connoisseur*, London, 1719. — Carlo RIDOLFI, *Le maraviglie dell'arte, overo Le vite de gl'illustri pittori veneti*, 2 vols., Venice, 1648; new edition by Detlev Freiherr von Hadeln, 2 vols., Berlin, 1914-1924. — H. RUHEMANN, *The Cleaning of Paintings: Problems and Potentialities*, London, 1968.

Joachim von SANDRART, *L'Academia todesca della architectura, scultura & pittura: oder, Teutsche Academie der Edlen Bau- Bild- und Mahlerey-Künste*, 3 vols., Nuremberg and Frankfurt, 1675-1679; edited by A. Peltzer, Munich, 1925. — Francesco SCANNELLI, *Il microcosmo della pittura*, Cesena, 1657; reprinted Milan, 1966. — L. SCARAMUCCIA, *Le finezze dei pennelli italiani*, Pavia, 1674; reprinted Milan, 1965. — Paul SIGNAC, *D'Eugène Delacroix au néo-impressionnisme*, Paris, 1899; edited by Françoise Cachin, Paris, 1964.

THEOPHILUS, *Libri III de diversis artibus; seu, Diversarum artium schedula*, Latin text, with English translation by Robert Hendrie, London, 1847. — Daniel V. THOMPSON, Jr., *The Materials of Medieval Painting*, foreword by Bernhard Berenson, New Haven, 1936; reprinted as *Materials and Techniques of Medieval Painting*, New York, 1958. — Théophile THORÉ-BÜRGER, *Salons de W. Bürger de 1861 à 1868*, 2 vols., Paris, 1870; *Les Salons (1844-1868). Etudes de critique et d'esthétique*, Paris, 1893.

Giorgio VASARI, *Le vite de' più eccellenti architetti, pittori et scultori italiani, da Cimabue insino a' tempi nostri*, 1st edition, 2 vols., Florence, 1550; *Le vite de' più eccellenti pittori, scultori e architettori*, 2nd enlarged edition, 3 vols., Florence, 1568; edited by Gaetano Milanesi, 9 vols., Florence, 1878-1885; English translation by Gaston du C. De Vere, 10 vols., London, 1912-1915; *Vasari on Technique*, translated by Louisa S. Maclehose, with introduction and notes by G. Baldwin Brown, London and New York, 1907, reprinted New York, 1960. — Lionello VENTURI, *Gusto dei primitivi*, Bologna, 1926; *History of Art Criticism*, translated by Charles Marriott, New York, 1936, 1964. — Johannes VIATOR (Jean PÉLERIN), *De artificiali prospectiva*, Toul, 1505. — J.G. VIBERT, *La science de la peinture*, Paris, 1925. — VILLARD DE HONNECOURT, *Facsimile of the Sketchbook of Wilars de Honecourt*, with commentaries and descriptions by J.B.A. Lassus and J. Quicherat, translated and edited by the Rev. Robert Willis, London, 1859; *Album de Villard de Honnecourt*, facsimile edition, Paris, 1906; *Kritische Gesamtausgabe des Bauhüttenbuches Ms. fr. 19093 der Pariser Nationalbibliothek*, edited by H.R. Hahnloser, Vienna, 1935.

J.J. WINCKELMANN, *Gedanken über die Nachahmung der griechischen Werke in der Malerei und Bildhauerkunst*, Dresden and Leipzig, 1755.

Alexandre ZILOTY, *La découverte de Jean van Eyck et l'évolution du procédé de la peinture à l'huile du Moyen Age à nos jours*, Paris, 1941; revised edition, Paris, 1947.

List of Illustrations

Paintings illustrated in the book only by
details are reproduced below in their entirety.
RMN = Réunion des Musées Nationaux, Paris.

A

B

C

D

E

F

G

O

P

R

S

T

Index of Names